To my GRE

LOVE, LIGHT, TRUTH, AND peace

Jack

THE PROCESS OF
Getting Ahead Sooner

AROUSE THE SLEEPING GREATNESS WITHIN YOU!

Jack Deurloo

BALBOA
PRESS
A DIVISION OF HAY HOUSE

Copyright © 2011 Jack Deurloo

All rights reserved. No part of this book may be used or reproduced by any means, graphic, electronic, or mechanical, including photocopying, recording, taping or by any information storage retrieval system without the written permission of the publisher except in the case of brief quotations embodied in critical articles and reviews.

Balboa Press books may be ordered through booksellers or by contacting:

*Balboa Press
A Division of Hay House
1663 Liberty Drive
Bloomington, IN 47403
www.balboapress.com
1-(877) 407-4847*

Because of the dynamic nature of the Internet, any web addresses or links contained in this book may have changed since publication and may no longer be valid. The views expressed in this work are solely those of the author and do not necessarily reflect the views of the publisher, and the publisher hereby disclaims any responsibility for them.

The author of this book does not dispense medical advice or prescribe the use of any technique as a form of treatment for physical, emotional, or medical problems without the advice of a physician, either directly or indirectly. The intent of the author is only to offer information of a general nature to help you in your quest for emotional and spiritual well-being. In the event you use any of the information in this book for yourself, which is your constitutional right, the author and the publisher assume no responsibility for your actions.

*Any people depicted in stock imagery provided by Thinkstock are models, and such images are being used for illustrative purposes only.
Certain stock imagery © Thinkstock.*

*ISBN: 978-1-4525-3563-0 (sc)
ISBN: 978-1-4525-3565-4 (hc)
ISBN: 978-1-4525-3564-7 (e)*

Library of Congress Control Number: 2011909908

Printed in the United States of America

Balboa Press rev. date: 06/23/2011

Dedication

I dedicate this book to my parents, Mr. & Mrs. Deurloo, now deceased. Thank you for your guidance, love and patience.

I love you both very much, now and always

I also dedicate this book to all my friends, students and seminar attendees who all suggested that I write this book.

Now that I am in the fall years of life I finally sat down and got pen to paper.

Thank you everyone for your love and encouragement.

Introduction

During my years of teaching (since 1976) I met many people who needed to make changes in their lives and who didn't know how to be successful.

Get out of your problems etc., etc. this book will give you the energy – the will and the power to control your lives and get the guidance you need to do this.

Contents

Dedication v
Introduction. vii
Acknowledgement xiii

Chapter 1   Let's Get Started 1

Chapter 2   What This Book Will Do For You 5

Chapter 3   Curiosity – That's the Secret 7
            My Own Story 10

Chapter 4   The Laws of Success. 13
            The Power of Thought. 14
            Will Is The Dynamic. 15
            You Can Control Your Destiny 16
            Fear Exhausts Life Energy 17
            A Wish is Desire Without Energy 18
            Failure Should Arouse Determination 19
            The Need for Self-Analysis! 20
            Habits of Thought Control One's Life. 21
            The Way of Meditation 23
            Success is Measured by Happiness. 24
            Facing Life!!! 26
            Contentment. 30
            Overcoming Procrastination 32
            Practicing Optimism! 33
            Enriching Our Lives!. 34
            Generate Enthusiasm! 35
            Believe. 36

Chapter 5	Thought	39
	Effect of Thought on Circumstances	41
	The Point of Power is the Present Moment	45
Chapter 6	Visualization & Imagination	47
	Visualization and Belief	51
Chapter 7	Unforgettable Henry J. Kaiser	53
	Mission Impossible	55
	A Mink for Mama	56
	Happy Elephant	58
	New Dealings	59
	Four-Wheel Flop	60
	Operation Retirement	62
Chapter 8	What Are You Afraid Of?	65
Chapter 9	Eight Steps to a New Life	71
Chapter 10	The Growth of Confidence	77
	You must make it a Positive Period	82
	Learn to repeat the Litany of your Faith	84
Chapter 11	The Monarch Butterfly	91
	How to Get the BEST Out of Life	93
	Finding What You Want	94
	The Eliminating Of Our Wants	95
	Learning to Talk, Trust and Feel!	96
	Expressing Joy!	97
	Take Time to Listen!	98
	Restoring Our Faith!	99
	Fitting In!	100
	Achieving Serenity!	101

Chapter 12	Communicating Clearly	103
	Developing Compassion!	104
	Shifting Our Outlook	105
	Turning The Worst Into The Best!	106
	Learning to Bend!	107
	Embracing Our Good!	109
Chapter 13	Success	111
	Motivation: The Driving Force	114
	Making a Good Brain Great!	116
	The Source	118
	Success Motivation	120
	85 Out of every 100 men	129
Chapter 14	"The Science"	131
	Brian & Linda	137
Chapter 15	Club La Vie	139
Chapter 16	Physically Hungry – Eat	145
	Mentally Hungry – What do you do?	146
	Do it Well – Subconsciously?	148
	Flea Trainer	151
Chapter 17	Tap – Tap – Tap!	153
	Use the Tap, Tap System!	156
	Harness Your Power to Faith	158
Chapter 18	Relaxation with Meditation	161
Chapter 19	Visualization and Imagination	165
	Visualization and Belief	169
	Visualization and Concentration	171
	The Art of Visualization	174

Chapter 20	Something to Think About	177
Chapter 21	Motivational/Inspirational Living	181
	Free Cruises	184
Chapter 22	My Own Sanctuary	187

Conclusion: My Comment to You!.................191

Acknowledgement

I am indebted to my many friends in both Canada and the United States, also my many students who have encouraged me to write this book. I will never forget my great friend Claire Ann Rochon who put all these pages in her computer from my long hand writing and corrected, proofread etc., etc. to make these pages come alive for you to read and grow!

With Love

Jack

• CHAPTER 1 •

Let's Get Started

As the title of this book says, it really gives you "a check-up" from the neck up.

In between your ears is this great computer, and as you know, you only get out of a computer what you put into a computer.

By most people the stuff between the ears is like a jelly mass, sitting there all clogged up, all you have put in there is your negative "stinking thinking". You're always complaining nothing is working right. You keep on complaining about work, your mate, your children, your neighbors and so called friends.

In other words, you are on the negative side of the street all the time. That is why I want to give you a "check-up" from the "neck-up". I'd like you to look up "check-up" in the dictionary, and you will read the meaning of their two words. It says something like inspection or examination or a patient going for their annual "check-up". This is what this book is all about. I want you to understand that there is a complete different world out there, from the one you live in. I am going to take all the negative crap out of your computer. I am changing this jelly mass between your ears and charging it up so you make something better of yourself. You are going to be in charge of your life. I will give you the roadmap to a much better destiny. I want to inspire you. I want to stir you and drive you to a better world. I call this motivation.

I hope that you still have your dictionary open. I want you to look up the word "motivation". It will say, "motivated to do something" or "to drive you to do something". Then I want you to look at "motivational". It will say something like "study of want conscious or sub-conscious influences, or actually induce people to a course of action".

The word "ELIMINATE" find it and it will stare you right in the face. To get rid of or to remove, expel waste and/or waste of time.

I want you to get back to the front of the dictionary and find "attitude". It will tell you something like, a way of thinking, feeling, behaving, change of attitude. We also look at enthusiasm. Many times we go through life dreaming and wishing that something good will come to you. We day dream often about this great job you'd like to have, this high score we'd like to achieve at the basketball court, this great car we'd like to drive, this beautiful vacation at some extreme place, our dream home, etc. etc.

In this book, I will show you that your wishbone can change to your backbone! I will prove to you, young and old, that all things are possible. Not just to other people but to you. This book will show you the way, and it is amazingly simple. You will say to yourself, "how come I never came across this before". I will give you this "check-up" from the "neck up" and change the jelly mass to good stuff. I will make your good brain – GREAT!!! Change your negative stinking thinking to enthusiasm. You will become a happier person. You will be motivated for your cause. People will show you respect. Your self-image will change. In a very short period of time your family, your friends, your place of work will see and feel the change in you. They will say, "Woooww, what happened, you changed".

The Princess of Getting Ahead Sooner

This is for all people of all ages and both sexes. Let's get to Chapter 2, and the excitement is going to start.

CHAPTER 2

What This Book Will Do For You

This book suggests techniques to you. I will demonstrate examples and personal experiences that you can use to become successful, improve your health and give you peace of mind and a constant flow of energy. Altogether, too many people are defeated by everyday problems in life. They feel down emotionally. They go on struggling or, perhaps whining, with a sense of resentment about the "bad breaks" that life has given them! It is quite unnecessary to feel defeated by your problems and go through hardships. It gives you a defeated attitude.

This writing is a direct and simple one. You have to see this as a simple and practical, direct-action, personal improvement manual. I am writing this to change your lifestyle and attitude to make you a better person and I will guide you to learn new ways of doing things that are good for you.

You bought this book because you needed and wanted change or improvement. The biggest room in the world is the room of improvement. You have to change your thoughts and things will change around you. Everything in life is created with thought. Look around and see all the material things around you; your furniture, your clothes, the kitchen, the carpet. Before it was created in material form, it was someone's creative "thought". A person saw it in a vision, daydreaming, invented etc., etc. Then it went on the drawing board or cutting table. Changes were made, design and creation took place and there we are with the material stuff that started with thought.

Everything is so creative, including happiness, unhappiness and attitude. You have to clear your mind of all the chaos that is in your head. Start thinking more clearly about what you need, in your life, to make yourself happy and successful. It is like a "movie of the mind". You are scripting your own movie. You are the director and the actor of your own future.

Begin this visualization by becoming deeply relaxed, using your own relaxation method. Allow yourself to relax your mind and body totally so that you are totally focused on your inner screen. When you feel yourself deeply relaxed, go to a place in your inner movie that is very beautiful and very peaceful. It might be a beach with waves gently billowing into the sand. Or it could be a lovely meadow on a glorious spring afternoon. It may even be a place where you have vacationed and been very happy and relaxed.

• CHAPTER 3 •

Curiosity – That's the Secret

The Quality that opens the door to all that life has to offer:
If you really work with determination at whatever you have to do, all sorts of things, that seem unconnected with your work, will be revealed to you. You find out about people; you find out about power, ambition, jealousy, weakness, love, compassion, hatred, failure, despair, generosity, meanness, the splendour of life and what is sometimes, the splendour of death. The whole pageant of life engulfs you, not only as a spectator, but, as an actor. Everything that life has to give you will be opened up to you through your work.

I hear you say: "He's mad!" You know people should have worked like demons for 45 years or more and at the age of 65 are left with nothing but a pension. Their jobs appear to have drained them of almost everything that they possessed. They were victims of, some will say, a cruel social system; others may say it was a lack of some sustaining belief; still others may say it was the barrenness of their cultural lives.

I think they were victims of themselves, first and foremost. They lacked a quality without which no life has any savour or great meaning. That quality is curiosity. Many years ago, a notable psychiatrist told me that curiosity was one of the most life-enhancing of human qualities – the cement that holds society together, the enricher and prolonger of human life. He was not joking. He saved literally hundreds of people every year who were in desperate straits because they had lost their curiosity.

I believe that if you bring curiosity to your work, it will cease to be merely a job and become a door through which you enter the best that life has to give to you. Let me give two examples: two men, both in Peterborough, ON, who brought immense curiosity to their jobs, who gave those jobs the best they had in them, and found in their lives that they were rick and influential. One of them, a teacher named FJA Morris, I never knew. I thing he was dead when I came to Peterborough, but, he was spoken of so often, and with such affection, that he was a living presence. He recognized that he was living in one of the great botanical areas in North America. The nearby Cavan Swamp was full of orchids. Everybody knew it, but nobody paid any particular attention until Morris explored the swamp with some of his pupils, and eventually wrote a book about the orchids there that became a classic of its kind. Thus he found a splendid world and opened it to others.

Morris was an educated man, but, another man whom I did now, Roy Powell, an electrician, was a man without much formal education. Roy was rather an eccentric. His method of determining whether or not electricity was coming through a socket was to lick his right thumb and stick it into the socket as far as it would go. If nothing happened, he would say: "Yep, she's dead." If blue fire came out of his elbow, he would smile and say: "Nope, she's okay."

But, sockets were not the centre of interest. He had been an early investigator of radio, and 60 years ago, he demonstrated in Peterborough that a model boat could be controlled by radio waves. When radio waves became a commonplace, he turned his attention to the study of optics, and loved making an optical toy. He invented an improvement on the simple kaleidoscope, and he used the make kaleidoscopes by the score and sends them to Toronto as gifts to the Hospital for Sick Children. Roy's conversation was fascinating, his curiosity boundless, and I think he was that extraordinary creature, a truly happy man.

Have I made my point? It is not work that kills, but, the narrowing of the spirit, the withering of the sympathies, the pinched nay saying response to life. The people who make work a door into the whole of the world live ALL their lives, and then live on in the memory of those they have warmed by the fire of their spirit. They give something we too may pass on to others, and in this way it may be said that the truth and force they brought to life never really die. This quality which I urge you to bring to your work and the world beyond it is the same quality that sustains and enlarges your inner life – that life from which everything you are takes its energy and its character.

My Own Story

When I was living in Cambridge, ON, I was operating a small painting business, in the middle of the seventies, I always been a newspaper reader and read it from cover to cover, as a matter of fact, I still do.

One day when I was going over the classified section, one ad stared right at me, and it said "Used appliances to pick-up for free", this ad got my curiosity in high gear. The next day I phoned the number in the ad, and got connected to the manager of the major appliances department of the store Simpson Sears, they were one company in the 70's, right now only the Sears store is operating and Simpson store was bought out, but that is another story altogether. Anyway the department manager mentioned that they sold new major appliances to customers, and would give their customer $100.00 for their old appliances but have to find a way to dispose of them on their own, of course not many people have trucks to bring them to the dump, so this is where the ad comes in, the store tried to help people to get rid of the appliances by advertising, "pick up appliances for free" the manager said that he had a couple of dozen people interested, but I asked him to put my name of the list, to do the pickups.

Nothing happened for about 3 weeks, then the department manager phones and said that there was a small office fridge to be picked up, of course, I went there, picked it up, in my station wagon, took it home, cleaned it up, had an electrician friend check it out and it was working perfectly, so I placed an ad in the paper and sold it for $60.00, while this was going on, another request came in for a fridge pick up, this one was in perfect working order, the reason the customer bought a new fridge was that they renovated the kitchen and the old fridge was too small to fill the size and location, so there I was with a perfect fridge which I sold for $120.00!

So you think this was great, this is only the beginning! Calls kept coming in and picking up I did, I had so many of them that I ran out of space, fridges, stoves, washers, dryers you name it I had them all, some good stuff, some junk. By now I rented an old warehouse behind a store in downtown Cambridge, it was dirty with dust, cobwebs, so I hosed it down, spray painted it, to make it clean and presentable and moved in all my used appliances. In the 70's there was a great shortage of appliance mechanics, so I phoned the apprenticeship program and was able to hire a man with a certificate right out of the apprenticeship program. He was a great guy and knew what he was doing.

A very good friend of mine was a fireman and a strong muscular man. He helped me with pick-ups and delivery, a good guy with a wonderful disposition and a people person. We sold a washer and dryer to a lady who was on Government Assistance Program, she was so happy with the installation, appliances and service that she told the Social Worker about this good business I was running. In about 2 months there were at least a dozen Social Workers sending people to us for used appliances. We had a motto, it has to be in "perfect working order" to sell, if not, junk it. And even the junk stuff returned some money; we brought it to the salvage yard, once a week. That gave us enough money to pay for the gasoline. I operated this used appliances business for two years, and then a man came to the shop a few times, looked around a little and left. He came by another time and said to me: "Jack you have a nice profitable business here." And I agreed with him, but playing it down a bit, saying something like: "and good staff, hard work and may hours of hard work..." He took me aside and offered me ten thousand dollars as an operating business. I declined his offer. A couple of weeks later he came back with his wife and talked about a deal again, and my answer was still no! Two days later he came again and handed me a twelve thousand dollar certified cheque, so he was not just talking, he backed it with money, and you all know "money" talks, and a few days after this I took my personal tools and work clothes out or the shop, shook hands with the new owner, wished him success and drove off.

When I write and talk about curiosity, I really live it, I am always curious about the world around me, why some people are successful and others fail. I believe "when you fail to plan, you plan to fail". Life will give you obstacles roadblocks, problems, but if you are strong enough and have fire in the belly, you will overcome them. Curiosity "that is the secret."

• CHAPTER 4 •

The Laws of Success

Is there a power that can reveal hidden veins of riches and uncover treasures of which we never dreamed of? Is there a force that we can all call upon to give us health, happiness, and spiritual enlightenment? The saints and sages of India teach that there is such a power. They have demonstrated the efficacy of truth principles that will work for you too if you give them a fair trial.

Your success in life does not altogether depend on ability and training; it also depends on your ability to grasp opportunities that are presented to you. Opportunities in life come by creation, not by chance. You yourself, either now or in the past, have created all opportunities that arise in your path. Since you earned your opportunities, use them to the best of your advantage.

When you have all available outward means, as well as your natural abilities to overcome every obstacle in your path, you will thus develop the powers of your higher self – unlimited power that flow from the innermost forces of your being. You possess the power of thought and the power of will. Use in life, to the uttermost, these divine gifts!!!

The Power of Thought

You demonstrate success or failure according to your habitual trend of thought. If your mind is ordinarily in a negative state, then occasional positive thought is not sufficient to attract success. But, when you think rightly, you will reach your goal even though you seem to be enveloped in darkness.

You alone are responsible for yourself. No one else may answer for your deeds when the final reckoning comes. Your work in the world, in the sphere where your karma (your own past activity) has placed you, can only be performed by one person – you. And your work can be called a "success" only when, in some way, it also serves your fellow man.

Don't mentally review any problem constantly. Let it rest at times and it may work itself out but see that you do not rest so long that your discrimination is lost. Rather, use these rest periods to go deep within the calm region of your inner self. Attune to your higher self. You will be able to think correctly regarding everything you do and, if your thoughts or actions have gone astray, they can be re-aligned. This power of divine atonement can be achieved by practice and effort.

Will Is The Dynamic

Along with positive thinking, you should use will-power and continuous activity in order to be successful. Every outward manifestation is the result of will, but this power is not always used consciously. There is mechanical will as well as conscious will. The dynamic of all your powers is volition, or will-power. Without volition, you cannot walk, talk, work, think, or feel. Therefore, will-power is the spring of all your actions. In order not to use this energy, you would have to be completely inactive both physically and mentally. Even when you move your hand, you are using will-power. It is impossible to live without using this force.

Mechanical will is an unthinking use of will-power. Conscious will is a vital force accompanying determination and effort, a dynamic that should be wisely directed as you train yourself to use your conscious, not mechanical will. You should also be sure that your will-power is being used constructively not for harmful purposes or for useless acquisitions.

To create dynamic will-power, determine to do some of the things in life that you thought you could not do. Attempt simple tasks first, as your confidence strengthens and your will-power becomes more dynamic, you can aim for more difficult accomplishments. Be certain that you have made a good selection then refuse to submit failure. Devote your entire will-power to mastering one thing at a time. Do not scatter your energies nor leave something half done to begin a new venture.

You Can Control Your Destiny

Your mind and subconscious are the creators of everything. You should therefore guide it to create only good. When you cling to a certain thought with dynamic will-power, it finally assumes a tangible outward form. When you are able to employ your will always for constructive purposes, you become the controller of your destiny.

I have just mentioned three important ways to make your will dynamic:

1. Choose a simple task or an accomplishment that you have never mastered and determine to succeed at it.

2. Be sure you have chosen something constructive and feasible and refuse to concede to failure. and,

3. Concentrate on a single purpose using all your abilities and opportunities to go forward with it.

You should always be sure within the calm region of your inner-self, that what you want is right for you to have and in accord with your higher sense of purpose. You can then use all the forces of your will to accomplish your objective. Keep your conscious and subconscious mind, however, centered on your dynamic thought force – the power of all accomplishments.

Fear Exhausts Life Energy

The human brain is a storehouse of life energy. This energy is constantly employed in muscular movements; in the working of the heart, lungs, diaphragm, etc. Besides this, a tremendous amount of life energy is required in all processes of thought, emotion and will.

Fear exhausts life energy. It is one of the greatest enemies of dynamic will-power. Fear causes the life force that ordinarily flows steadily, through the nerves, to be squeezed out and the nerves themselves to become as though paralyzed. The vitality of the whole body is lowered. Fear doesn't help you to get away from the subject of fear, it only weakens your will-power. Fear causes the brain to send an inhibiting message to all body organs. It constricts the heart, the digestive functions, and causes many other physical disturbances. When the conscious and subconscious stick to "the science", every obstacle will then be overcome by a faith in yourself.

A Wish is Desire Without Energy

After a wish may come to your intention, the plan to do a thing, to fulfill a wish of desire, but "will" means I act until I get my wish".

When you exercise your will power, you release the power of life energy, not when you merely wish passively to be able to obtain an objective.

Failure Should Arouse Determination

Even failures should act as stimulants to your will power and to your material and spiritual growth. When you have failed in any project, it is helpful to analyze every factor in the situation in order to eliminate all chances in the future that you might repeat the same errors.

The season of failure, is the best time for sowing the seeds of success. The bludgeon of circumstances may bruise you, but keep your head up erect. Always try "once more", no matter how many times you have failed. Fight when you think that you can fight no longer, or when you think that you have already done your best or until your efforts are crowned with success!!

New efforts after failure bring true growth, but they must be planned and charged with increasing intensity of attention and with dynamic will power. The successful person may have had more serious difficulties to contend with than one who has failed; but the former trained himself / herself to reject the thought of failure all the time.

You should transfer your attention from failure to success, from worry to calmness, from mental wandering to concentration, from restlessness to peace, from peace to the divine bliss within. When you attain this state of self-realization the purpose of your life has been gloriously fulfilled.

The Need for Self-Analysis!

Another secret of progress is self-analysis. Introspection is a mirror in which to see recesses of your mind that otherwise would remain hidden from you. Diagnose your failures and sort out your good and bad tendencies. Analyze what you are, what you would like to become, and what shortcomings are impeding you. Decide the nature of your true task, your mission in life. Endeavour to make yourself what you should be and what you want to be. As you keep your mind on your subconscious mind and attune yourself accordingly, you will progress more and more surely in your path. Your ultimate purpose is to find your way back to the task at hand and perform to your outer world. Will power combined with initiative will help you to recognize and fulfill your goal.

Habits of Thought Control One's Life

Success is hastened or delayed by one's habits. It's not your passing inspiration or brilliant ideas so much as your everyday mental habits that control your life. Habits of thought are mental magnets that draw to you certain things, people and conditions. Good habits of thought enable you to attract benefits and opportunities. Bad habits of thought attract you to bad people and bad situations.

Weaken a bad habit by avoiding everything that occasioned it, or stimulated it, without concentrating on it in your zeal to avoid it. Then divert your mind to some good habits and steadily cultivate it until it becomes a part of you.

There are always two forces warring against each other within us. One force tells us to do things we should not do, and the other urges us to do things we should do, the things that seem difficult. One voice is bad and the other voice is that of good. Through difficult, daily lessons you will see sometime clearly that bad habits nourish the tree of unending desires while good habits nourish the tree of aspirations. More and more you should concentrate your efforts on successfully nurturing the spiritual tree, that you may someday gather the ripe fruit of self-realization.

When you are able to free yourself from all kinds of bad habits and if you are able to do good because you want to do good and not merely because bad brings sorrow, then you are truly progressing in the right direction.

It is only when you discard your bad habits that you are really a "free" man or woman. Until you are a true master, able to command yourself to do the things that you should do but may not want to do, you are not a free person. In the power of self-control lies the seed of eternal freedom.

I have now mentioned several important attributes of success; positive thoughts, dynamic will, self-analysis, initiative, and self-control. Many popular books stress one or more of these, but fail to give credit to the divine power behind them. Atonement to the divine will-power (your higher self) is the most important factor in attracting success.

The Way of Meditation

After you have repaired your mental radio and are clearly attuned to constructive vibrations, how may you use it to reach your goals? The right method of meditation is the way (see Chapter on meditation).

By the power of concentration (the science method) and meditation you can direct the inexhaustible power of the mind to accomplish what you desire and to guard every door against failure.

All successful men and women devote much time to deep concentration. They are able to dive deeply within their mind and to find the pearls of right solutions for the problems that confront them. When you learn how to withdraw your attention from all objects of distraction and to place it upon one object of concentration, you too will know how to attract at will whatever you need.

Before embarking on important undertakings, sit quietly, calm your senses and thoughts, and meditate deeply. You will then be guided by the great creative power of your subconscious. After that, you should utilize all necessary material means to achieve your goals.

The things you need in life are those that help you to fulfill your dominant purpose. Things you may want but not need lead you aside from that purpose. It is only by making everything serve your main objective that success is attained.

Success is Measured by Happiness

Consider whether fulfillment of the goal you have chosen will constitute success, what is success?

If you possess health and wealth but have trouble with everybody (including yourself), yours is not a successful life. Existence becomes futile if you cannot find happiness. When wealth is lost, you have lost little; when your health is lost, you have lost something of more consequence; but when peace of mind is lost, you have lost the highest treasure.

Success should therefore be measured by the yardstick of happiness; by your ability to remain in peaceful harmony with your conscious and subconscious mind. Success is not rightly measured by the worldly standards of life, prestige and power. None of these gives you happiness unless they are rightly used. To use them rightly one must possess wisdom and love for all mankind and the universe.

You have the power to reward or punish yourself by the use or misuse of your own reason and will-power. When you transgress the laws of health, prosperity, and wisdom you must inevitably suffer sickness, poverty and ignorance. However, you should strengthen your mind and refuse to carry the burden of mental and moral weaknesses acquired in past years. Burn them in the fires of your present divine resolutions and right activity. By this constructive attitude you will attain freedom and happiness.

Happiness depends to some extent upon external conditions but chiefly upon your own mental attitudes. In order to be happy one should have good health, a well balanced mind, a prosperous life, the right kind of work a thankful heart, and above all, wisdom and knowledge in your higher self.

A strong determination to be happy will help you. Do not wait for your circumstances to change, thinking falsely that in them lies the trouble. Do not make unhappiness a chronic habit, thereby afflicting yourself and those you love. It is a blessing for yourself and others when you are happy. It will affect everything in your life and those you touch.

Facing Life!!!

Sooner or later everyone arrives at a point where life seems to have become too big to cope with. Life is never really too much for us but it can seem to be, when this happens we have to get life back in focus. We have lost our perspective but it can be regained.

You may have come to think of the world as unspeakably fast. The earth, twenty-five thousand miles around, outer space, full of unknown worlds. But actually, the world is limited in your home, your shop, your work, your family and your town or city. Even if you fly to Amsterdam, South Korea or Moscow, your world is no bigger than the interior of the airplane and no further away than the nearest airport.

You may have come to regard the world as teeming with millions of people. In reality, your world consists of a very small number of people – those you life with, those you work with and those you're acquainted with. And the awful, menacing future, that unending nightmare of shadowy days and years! Can't even bear to think about it? Well, quit thinking about it all. You live only a split second at a time – that's right this minute! You can only think of one thing at a time, do only one thing at a time. You actually live only one breath at a time. So stop living in tomorrow it may never come and start living only one day at a time. Plan for tomorrow but live only till bedtime comes tonight. So, in short, that big Bogeyman – life – can be cut down to its real size. Life is only this place, this time, and these people right here and now. This you can handle – at least for today. "But my life is just one problem after another!" Of course it is! ....That's life!

I don't know how it is with you, but it took me a long time to realize that at least some of these problems were of my own making. For instance, I thought that it was my duty to solve other people's problems, arbitrate their disputes and show them how to live their lives. I was hurt when they rejected my unsolicited advice. I finally learned that you cannot help people unless they really need help, are willing to be helped, want you to help them and ask you to help them. Even then, you can only help them to help themselves.

An old Arab whose tent was pitched next to a company of whirling dervishes was asked, "Don't they bother you?" "No", the Arab answered. "What do you do about them"? He was asked. "I let 'em whirl!"

I caused myself a lot of unnecessary grief by trying to be unselfish, to think of everybody first, myself last and to try to please everybody. But you can't please everybody. You can knock yourself out doing this and that and the other thing to please "your cousins and your sisters and your brothers and your aunts" only to find out that they were not affected one way or another. Remember – please everybody – nobody's pleased, please yourself, at least you are pleased!

Charity begins at home. Enlightened self-interest is a basic endowment of human nature. You can save yourself a lot of grief by admitting the futility of trying to please everybody or trying to please somebody who just can't be pleased.

A surprising number of people believe that other people can hurt their feelings. They won't believe you when you tell them that it just isn't so and that no one can hurt you unless you let them. If irresponsible or unreasonable criticism causes you unhappiness, that is at least partly your own fault. We all say, "I don't care what people say!" But the tragic thing is that we do care and pretending we don't makes things worse. What do we do? Practice turning a deaf ear to the person who irritates or upsets you. Make up your mind that you are not going to let yourself pay attention to what 'he' or 'she' says and mean it. This you won't believe until you try it. If you refuse at least to try it, some suspicious or cynical soul might suspect that perhaps, you've got so in the habit of having your feelings hurt that you'd be bored otherwise. So much for unnecessary suffering! How about real trouble? Trouble that comes regardless of what we do, think or say? That terrifying problem that has no apparent solution? Let's stop for a minute and see what the problem really is.

A problem is a set of circumstances that threaten your well-being. And what are circumstances?

Circumstances are people or things. So "solving our problems" really means getting people and things the way we want them. Sometimes we can do it, more often we can't. What then? There are several things we can do. We can look around to find somebody or something to blame. Or we can put ashes in our hair, wear shabby shoes with rundown heels, accentuate our wrinkles and make the rounds of our friends chanting, "poor, poor me"! We can succeed in making our family miserable. We can haunt doctors. We can waylay our pastor, beat our chest and blame God, "what have I done to deserve this!? These various 'home remedies' – blaming everybody, self-pity, and the rest have but one result: they make everybody, including ourselves, more miserable and add to our difficulties without solving them.

Do what the politician does, if you can't beat them, join them. When you don't solve your problems, learn to live with them and in spite of them.

Oh sure, just like that! Very simple, my friend. So simple you wouldn't try it unless you were desperate. When you are desperate enough, you'll try anything. So try something that works. Try acceptance!

Acceptance is the only real source of tranquility, serenity and peace of mind. It is also known as 'surrender', 'bowing to the inevitable', and 'joining them'. It can be acquired if you have an urgent desire to help yourself and are willing to ask your subconscious mind to help.

Luckily for us, the perfect formula for acceptance, simple and practical as a can opener, is ready at hand, waiting for us to use, as hundreds of thousands before us have. Your mind is like a parachute, it only works when it opens.

Here is the serenity prayer, written a long time ago:

God grant me the serenity to accept the things I cannot change,
The courage to change the things I can, and
The wisdom to know the difference.

Contentment

Baby screams because mama won't let the baby play with the nice, big, shiny butcher knife. Baby is very unhappy. He can't have what he wants and he doesn't want that silly old rattle. Baby has yet to learn that contentment lies not in getting what he wants by enjoying what he has.

When we grown-ups are contented only when we are getting what we want, we're going to be discontented most of the time. That way, our happiness depends on circumstances over which we have no control. No human being is so wise and powerful that he or she can control circumstances. Then we had better see what we can do about finding our own enjoyment. Since we can't get everything we want, we must learn to enjoy what we have. Well, what have you? You are alive and you have six senses in more or less good working order. Even if you were deaf, dumb and blind, you could at least take enjoyment from the sensation of breathing.

I am not deaf, dumb or blind. I can even look at a smouldering turd and enjoy the realization that I can see it and smell it. I can listen to a cat yowling outside my window at three a.m. and enjoy the realization that there is nothing wrong with my hearing. I can walk. I can enjoy the sensation of picking up my feet and putting them down. I can be colorblind and still enjoy a little baby's gurgling. As a matter of fact, we can find something enjoyable in any situation, no matter how disagreeable, when we look for it. When we try hard enough we can even enjoy the drudgery of our work.

The Process of Getting Ahead Sooner

Don't make the mistake of postponing your enjoyment until vacation time or even the weekend. Some people have to go to the movies or nightclubs for amusement and laughs. When their own children can provide more than enough amusement. Let's enjoy here and now!

Perhaps the most difficult thing to bear is loneliness. What to do when circumstances force us into a solitary existence? First, when you are fortunate enough to have a variety of interests, physical or mental, you must make a real effort to develop them. Failing that, you can search out and help the less fortunate. If you are not up to that, you are thrown back on the conscious cultivation of your own six senses and intellectual powers. At the very least, you can tell your subconscious mind that you hold yourself available for good things to come.

Overcoming Procrastination

Putting things off can eat away at us. Underneath procrastination is the fear of not being perfect at what we do. We become so preoccupied with perfection that we cannot get started on what needs accomplishing. So we do things to distract us from the task while worrying about getting the job done well. Our long list and delay, piles up shores of weight on our shoulders. Procrastination increases our anxiety and irritability.

The first step is to distinguish between essentials and non essentials. Work through our priorities one at a time. By putting one foot in front of the other complete just one task at a time. We will feel less defeated and more hopeful about our day. The burden of procrastination lifts as we do what needs doing, one task at a time, without worrying about the mountain of non essentials.

Practicing Optimism!

At first, the tourist was smitten by the beauty of the country. But after a week, his appreciation of the beauty was marred by his attention to the garbage in the river and the cracks in the pavement. As an experience becomes familiar, we begin to lose the fresh outlook that we started with. But turning dislikes into preferences and negative attitude into positive ones can transform our mental outlook.

Practicing optimism keeps life fresh and develops within us a deeper appreciation for the blessings we have. Living each day as if it's our first can transform our lives. As we experience our lives through fresh eyes, we find that our days are richer and fuller and we are more content with the world around us. The following affirmation can help:

Today, I expect to be awestruck as I experience my life through fresh eyes and attitude. I am deeply appreciative of my life and the people in it. Today is the first day in my life, yesterday is a cancelled cheque!!

Enriching Our Lives!

Self-doubt keeps us from taking necessary risks for personal growth. When we open ourselves to a person, we take this risk of being rejected or being criticized for expressing our opinions. To escape criticism, we learn to do nothing, say nothing, and be nothing.

We can employ faith and trust to go before us so that mistrust, fear and pessimism are cleared from our path. When we want to get somewhere, we take action and move, after leaving ourselves vulnerable, facing risk and criticism and going against fear. Taking risks and being open to change are essentials to enriching our lives.

The only way we can get fruit from the tree is to go out on a limb. When we can choose to do one thing differently, or one we have never done before, no matter how small, then we can stand back and watch ourselves grow.

Generate Enthusiasm!

There are days when we dread getting out of bed. It may be a day with back to back appointments or a day when we feel we cannot face an enraged co-worker. We may be overcome with anxiety about speaking in front of a large group of people. We may simply be burned up from a long commute from work to home. Or it just may be raining again.

There are eight hours between nine to five. That's a lot of time to muster enthusiasm. We start with putting one foot in front of the other. We refuse to let flimsy excuses keep us from home.

We look for one thing in the day, no matter how small, that will bring a tinge of excitement. We compliment one person we see in the morning, smile at another and look through the usual for something extraordinary. By the end of the day we have turned the early morning dread into enthusiasm simply by changing our attitudes!

Believe

As I said before, success is a *belief*, a *belief* that you will succeed. When you want to be successful, you need to know exactly what you want and where you are going. You have to tell your subconscious mind what you need. If you don't have direction and don't have a plan and have a vague idea of what you want and need, settle down and lay out a plan. Tell your subconscious mind about your future plans. Make sure you use the "card science" and things will come. Small needs will come first. Large plans will come step by step.

Remember, Rome was not built in a day. Give your subconscious mind detailed instructions, be positive, the more detailed, the more likely you are to attract the success you want. It is important to be really motivated by what you need and believe worthy for success to come to you. Enjoy it, self-talk about it, visualize it and then commit yourself to the plan.

Sometimes, right out of the blue, comes the answer of how to proceed next. The longest road trip is still done one mile at a time. A friend of mine and myself drove down from Toronto to Baja, Mexico. A long, long ride, one mile at a time. On the way, we got a flat tire. To us it was only a "hiccup" because the rest of the trip went great! What I mean to say is that, yes, there will be a road block or a "hiccup" sometimes, on the road to success. But, if you are the person that I think you are, you will overcome it. You can also go around it, or overtop of it, or under it. I know you have the power, the instinct, the fortitude, the insight to do it! To quote Obama's line, "Yes, you can!"

The Process of Getting Ahead Sooner

When I had my business in Toronto, it was a very active place. I taught motivational seminars. My secretary, who worked for me for many years, knew me very well. On my birthday in 1977, she gave me a wall plaque with the following message written on it:

Success is failure turned inside out,
The silver tint of the clouds of doubt,
And you never can tell how close you are.
It may be nearer when it seems afar,
So stick to the fight when you're hardest hit.
It's when things seem worse you mustn't quit!

It was signed, "Love Bonnie".

She gave this to me because of the way I talk, walk and live.

Of course I was very excited to get this wonderful birthday present and, as a matter of fact, I have it hanging on the wall in the front entrance of my apartment.

CHAPTER 5

Thought

You've all heard the saying, "As a man thinketh, so is he". In other words, we are happy or unhappy as a result of our thoughts mankind is made or unmade by their army of thoughts, we forge the weapons by which we destroy ourselves; but also fashion the tools with which we build ourselves heavenly mansions of joy, strength and peace. By the right choice and true applications of thought, men and women ascend to perfection; by the abuse and wrong application of thought, he or she descends below the level of the beast. Between these two extremes are all the grades of character and mankind is the master maker.

Of all the beautiful truths pertaining to the soul which have been restored and brought to light in this age, none is more gladdening and fruitful of divine promise and confidence than this – that mankind is the master of thought, the moulder and the maker and the shaper of conditions, environmental and destiny.

As a being of power, intelligence and love, and the boss of his or her thoughts, we hold the key to every situation and contain within ourselves the transforming and regenerating agency which we may make ourselves what we will.

You are always the master, even in your weakest and most abandoned state, but in this weakness and degradation, you are the masters who misgovern your "household". When you begin to reflect upon your condition and to search diligently by the law upon which your "being" is established, you then become the wise master directing your energies with intelligence and fashioning your thoughts to fruitful issues, such as the subconscious master, and mankind can only thus become by discovering within themselves the laws of thought; which discovery is totally a matter of applications, self-analysis and experiences.

Only by much searching and mining are gold and diamonds obtained, and mankind can find truth connected with their being. If he or she will dig deep into the mind and his or her soul; and that they understand that they are the makers of their own character, the moulders of their lives and the builders of their destiny, then they may unerringly prove, if they watch, control and alter their thoughts, tracing their efforts upon themselves, upon others and upon their life circumstances, linking cause and effect by patient practice and investigations, and utilizing their every experiences, even to the most trivial, everyday occurrences as a means of obtaining that knowledge for themselves which is understanding, wisdom and power. In this direction, as in no other, is the law of absolute. For only by patience, practice and ceaseless opportunity can mankind reach their goal.

Effect of Thought on Circumstances

A man or woman's mind may be likened to a garden. It may be intelligently cultivated or allowed to run wild. But whether cultivated or neglected, it must and will grow food or grow weeds. When no useful seeds are put into the soil, then an abundance of weeds will grow and will produce their kind. Just as a gardener cultivates his plot, keeping it free from weeds and growing the flowers and fruits which he requires, so may a man or woman tend the garden of their mind and subconscious mind, weeding out all the useless and impure thoughts and cultivating toward perfection, the flowers and fruits or right, useful and pure thought. By pursuing this process a person, sooner or later, discovers that they are the master gardeners of their lives and director of their lives. They also reveal, within themselves, the laws of thought and understanding with ever increasing accuracy. How the thought forces and mind elements operate in the shaping of their character, circumstances and destiny.

Thought and character are one and as character can only manifest and discover itself through environment and circumstances the outer conditions of a person's life will always be found to be harmoniously related to their inner state. This does not mean that a person's circumstances at any given time are an indication of entire character, but that these circumstances are so intimately connected with some vital thought element within ourselves that for the time being, they are indispensable to his or her own development.

• JACK DEURLOO •

Every person is where they are by law of their being. The thoughts which they have built in their character have brought them there and in the arrangement of their life there is no element of change. All is the result of a law which cannot err. This is just as true of those who feel "out of harmony" with their surroundings as of those who are contented with them. As a progressive and evolving being, a person is where they are so that they may learn to grow. As they learn the spiritual lessons which any circumstance contains for the, it passes away and gives the way to other circumstances.

Mankind if buffeted by circumstances so long as they believe themselves to be the creature of outside conditions, but when they realize that they are the creative power and that they may commend the hidden soil and seeds of their being, out of which circumstances grow, they then become the rightful master of themselves.

Circumstances grow out of thoughts, every man and woman who has practiced self control and self purification knows, for they will have noticed that the alteration in their circumstances has been in exact ratio with their altered mental condition. So true is this that when mankind earnestly applies themselves to remedy their defects in character and makes swift and marked progress, they pass rapidly through a succession of vicissitudes.

The soul attracts that which is secretly harbours; that which it loves and also that which it fears, the height of its' cherished aspirations, it falls to the level of its' unchastened desires and circumstances are the means which the soul receives its' own.

Every thought-seed sown or allowed to fall into the mind, and to take root there, produces its own blossoming, sooner or later, bearing its' own fruitage or opportunity and circumstances. Good thoughts bear good fruit, bad thoughts bear bad fruit.

The outer world of circumstances shapes itself to the inner world of thought and both pleasant and unpleasant external conditions are factors which make for the ultimate good of the individual. As the reaper of his own harvest, mankind learns by suffering and bliss.

Men and women do not attract that which they want but that which they are! Their whims, fancies and ambitions are thwarted at every step but their innermost thoughts and desires are fed with their own food, be it clean or foul.

"The divinity that shapes our ends" is in us. It is our very own selves. Men and women are manacled only by themselves. By thought and action they imprison themselves. They are also the angles of freedom. Not by what they wish for and pray for do men and women get but what he or she justly earn. Their wishes and prayers are only gratified and answered when they harmonize with their thought force and action. In the light of this truth, what then is the meaning of "fighting against circumstances? It means that men and women are continually revolting against an effect while all the while they are nourishing and preserving it's' cause in his or her own head. That unconscious weakness stubbornly retards the efforts of its' possessor and thus calls out for a remedy. People are anxious to improve their circumstances but are unwilling to improve themselves. They therefore remain bound!

Even the person whose sole objective is to acquire wealth must be prepared to make great personal sacrifices before he or she can accomplish his or her objective. And how much more they would realize a strong and well poised life! Consider a person who is wretchedly poor and extremely anxious that their surroundings and home comforts should be improved. Yet, all the time they shirk their work and feel they are justified in trying to deceive their employer on the ground of the insufficiency of their wages. Such a person does not understand the simplest rudiments of those principles which are the basis or true prosperity and it's not only totally unfitted to rise out of their predicament but is actually attracting to themselves a still deeper problem by dwelling in and acting out insolent, deceptive and underhanded thoughts.

Consider a rich man who is the victim of a painful and persistent disease as the result of gluttony. He is willing to pay large sums of money to get rid of this disease but is not willing to give up his gluttonous desires. He wants to gratify his taste for rich and unnatural ways and have his health as well. Such a man is totally unfit to have health because he has not yet learned the first principles of a healthy life.

Consider an employer who adopts crooked measures to avoid paying the regular wages and in hopes of making large profits, reduces the wages of his employees. Such an employer is altogether unfit for prosperity and when he finds himself bankrupt, both in riches and in reputation, he blames circumstances not realizing or accepting that he is the sole author of his condition.

I have introduced these three cases merely to illustrate the truth that mankind is the cause of his or her circumstances and that while aiming at a good end, they are continually frustrating its accomplishments by encouraging thoughts and desires which cannot possibly harmonize with that end. Such cases can be multiplied and varied almost indefinitely but this is not necessary as the reader can, when they resolve to trace the action of the laws of thought in their own mind and life and until this is done, mere external facts cannot serve as a ground of reasoning.

The Point of Power is the Present Moment

The point of power is the present moment right here and right now in our minds. It does not matter how long we have had negative patterns or an illness or a rotten relationship or a lack of finances or self hatred. We can begin to make a change today! The thoughts we have held and the words we have repeatedly used have created out life and experiences up to this point. Yet, that is past thinking. We have already done that. What we are choosing to think and say today, in this moment, will create tomorrow and the next day and the next week and the next month and the next year. The point of power is always in the present moment! This is where we begin to make changes. What a great liberating idea! We can and should begin today to let the old nonsense go. Right here and now, promise yourself to change! The smallest beginning will make a difference.

When you were a tiny baby you were pure joy and love. You knew how important you were. You felt you were the centre of the universe. You have courage. You asked for what you wanted and you expressed all your feelings openly. You loved yourself totally and knew you were perfect. That is the truth of your being. All the rest is learned nonsense and can be unlearned. How often have you said, "That's the way I am" or "that's the way it is"? What you are really saying is that it is what we believe to be true for us. Usually what we believe is only someone else's opinion that we have accepted and incorporated into our own belief system. When we were taught as children that the world is a frightening place, then everything we hear that fits in with that belief is accepted as true for us. "Don't talk with strangers", Don't go out at night", "People cheat on you, etc., etc. On the other hand, when we are taught early in life that the world is a safe and joyous place, then we would believe other things, "Love is everywhere", "People are so friendly", "Money comes to me so easily" and so on.

Life experiences mirror our beliefs. We seldom sit down and question our beliefs. For instance, I could ask myself, "why do I believe it is difficult for me to learn?", "Is that really true?", "Is it true for me now?", "Where did that belief come from?", "Do I still believe in that because a fifth grade teacher told me over and over?", "Would I be better off if I dropped that belief?", etc., etc. Stop for a moment and catch your thoughts. What are you thinking right now? What are you thinking right this moment? When thoughts shape your life and experiences, would you want this thought to become true for you? If it is a thought of worry or anger or hurt or revenge, how do you think this thought will come back to you? When we want joyous life, we must think joyous thoughts. Whatever we send out mentally or verbally will come back to us in like form!

Take a little time to listen to the words we say. If you hear yourself saying something three times write it down. It has become a pattern for you. At the end of a week, look at the list you have made and you will see how your words fit your experiences. Be willing, from now on, to change your words and your thoughts and watch your life change! The way to control your life is to control your choice of words and thoughts. No one thinks in your mind but you. Don't forget, your mind is like a parachute, it only works when it opens!

· CHAPTER 6 ·

Visualization & Imagination

We noted that the very first step toward personal motivation is to crystallize your thinking so that you know where you stand now and where you are going. But without some further amplification of what is meant by "crystallized thought", your success may fall short of your expectations. Our world moves at such a rapid pace that much of our thinking is done in vague generalities. We read or we listen to what others have to say with varying degrees of receptivity.

The moment our minds grasp a general understanding of one idea, we proceed to the next one. There is seldom any dialogue that helps fix the outlines of these thoughts with any exact definition or boundary. Our minds do not expand to encompass the whole idea – there just isn't enough time. As a result, our thought is seldom crystallized to the point that we know exactly what we have heard or read. We form the habit of generalizing ideas.

When you resolve to fill out a plan of action for your life – you begin to analyze where you stand and where you are going – generalizations do not suffice. Your ideas and thoughts should be able to see not only the goals, but every step you will take to reach them without one moment of hesitation or uncertainty. And the way you achieve this kind of crystallized thinking is through the process of visualization.

In our culture today, virtually all patterns of thought are geared to sight. The simplest thought usually calls forth an image in the mind's eye. Mention a tree and one "sees" a tree. Mention an abstract thought and the mind must grapple with it until it is able, somehow, to reduce the abstraction to a mental picture. When a person is unable to "get the picture", he/she is confused and does not understand. Or, if he/she gets a wrong picture, he/she misunderstands. That, in a very literal sense, is visualization. In other words, we relate the present to the past by converting current thoughts into mental pictures of our past experiences, and we understand by association. We form a "bridge" by using visualization.

Mankind does not use visualization to his/her best advantage, however, until he/she develops the art of visualization in its highest form: that of relating the present to the *future*. When he/she is able to use his/her powers to relate the "what is" to the "what can be", he/she has developed visualization into a genuine art.

To illustrate that you have the basic ability to visualize, I ask you to think of an automobile. Your mind will picture that idea very quickly. But, if you're like most people, the picture you get is rather hazy. If I ask you to describe the automobile you have in mind, you've got to go back and refocus the picture because you didn't really know, in the beginning, what to expect. And even when you've got a mental picture so clear that you can describe the car, it's pretty sure that the car you see is your own car. That's the way most of us respond to the little events in our life. Our minds are lazy and we get by on minimum requirements of effort. We restrict our visualization to that which we already know – to the familiar and commonplace. We omit imagination, the spice that adds meaning and zest to our power of visualization.

The successful people – the self-motivated people – are not restricted. They have set their imagination free. They know that they can visualize anything that they can create, *and* that they can create anything that they visualize. They have found, by the process of visualization, they can move the future into the present and greatly expand their own experiences. They get the jump on tomorrow. They are prepared for it because they are already "familiar" with it. They have already "seen" it through visualization.

Almost everyone is adept at bridging the past with the present. That's how we profit from past experiences. And we do so with some confidence and self-assurance. But, how much more confidence would we have if we extended our ability and utilized the practice to give us the same understanding of our future actions? Vivid imagination makes this kind of visualization possible. A person must be able to unshackle themselves, set their emotions free and be willing to sense each experience they visualize. When they can taste, smell, hear, or touch, as well as, see regarding the future, their imagination is most vivid.

The top teaching professions in the world of golf tell their students that one of the most important secrets of making a golf shot is being able to visualize where you want the ball to go. They stress the importance of seeing in the mind's eye the exact flight path of the ball. If one can also hear the click of the ball and feel the smooth flex of the muscles, his/her chances of making the shot are virtually assured. Why? Because the thought is the data fed into the computer, the brain, and the entire body chemistry gets the message clearly. The muscles respond according to precise instructions. A person's timing, body control and swing come almost automatically because visualization has commanded that they respond appropriately. By contrast, if a person is confused – if they don't know which club to use or how they want the shot to look – their computer feeds garbled messages to the muscles and the shot is missed. Anyone who has played the game for a period of years knows this principle to be true. Yet it is not a principle confined to the sports world, in general, not to golf in particular. It is a pragmatic principle available to anyone in any profession and it is especially effective as you crystallize your thinking about what you want to achieve in life.

Visualization and Belief

All of us are familiar with the old saying "seeing is believing", but that statement was never more true than when it is related to visualization. When a person sets certain goals, aims and desires, and when they use their power of visualization to picture themselves already in possession of those goals, they develop an almost miraculous belief in themselves and their ability to achieve those goals.

Far too many people make resolutions, or set goals for attitude changes but rely solely on their willpower to accomplish the objective. Willpower alone will not work because our determination and willpower do not foster *belief*. Unless we can "see" the end results through visualization, we are forging ahead into the "unknown" and our confidence and belief will not sustain us. The reason so many find it difficult to lose weight or stop smoking, or break any long ingrained habit, is because they rely solely on willpower.

Remember that habits and attitudes are changed by displacement. A person must find a more satisfactory mode of behaviour to replace the old habits. This can be done by visualizing oneself already having the new behaviour. This is not to say that determination isn't important. It *is* important, as we shall see. It does not provide any new or more satisfactory mode of action, and it does not bolster belief.

The role visualization plays in fostering the belief that attitudes can be changed prompts us to make a comparison between genuine visualization and daydreams. The two should never be confused because in almost every respect they are direct opposites. Daydreams are an escape from the pressures of reality. Visualization is a constructive way to meet the challenges of life head-on and overcome them. Daydreams are spawned in the inactive. The daydreamer never intends to take action on their daydreams. The person who develops his/her power of visualization does so with purpose. They not only plan to act but are also practicing the art so that they will be prepared to act more effectively. The daydreamer does not believe in what he/she dreams. Their dream is only a whim, a wish, a fantasy. Many times they would not even want the dream to come true if they had the power to make it so. The person of vision develops belief, confidence and assurance that what they see is not only possible but is in fact in the process of becoming reality. They are on their way, and in a sense, they have already arrived because they have pre-tasted the satisfaction of achieving it. They use their power of visualization like the picture editor of a magazine such as *Life, Look or National Geographic*. They select the pictures they want, carefully, and build the "story" or their personal development around them. At the same time, they reject and discard those pictures they do not want. Their editorial policy sets out a constructive course of action for them to follow. They learn to distinguish the true from the false, the real from the unreal. When problems and obstacles confront them like a wall, they know that they have only to raise their sights higher to find a way around or over any hindering circumstances. The person who can visualize is well on their way to success because they have seen the progressive realization of their predetermined worthwhile goals.

• CHAPTER 7 •

Unforgettable Henry J. Kaiser

He and I had a game we liked to play. Sitting at dinner, I would propose some building project, the more farfetched the better.

"Could you build a bridge across the English Channel?" I would ask. His round, Buddha-like face would bread into a broad grin. His shrewd eyes would widen as if in wonder, rather than narrowing as most men's do when they calculate a problem. His 6'2", 250 lb body would squirm in his chair and his jowls would quiver.

"Yes" he would finally announce with satisfaction. "We can do it." And then he'd tell me how. Nothing was impossible to Henry J. Kaiser. He helped build the Hoover, Grand Coulee and Bonneville dams, and the San Francisco-Oakland Bay Bridge. During World War II his shipyards turned out 1440 Liberty cargo ships and 50 baby aircraft carriers for the U.S. war effort. Although he was a grade school dropout, his empire, at his death embraced 196 plants and facilities in 34 countries, employed 90,000 people and grossed two billion dollars a year. He also built the 19 Kaiser hospitals and 45 clinics which today serve nearly two million subscribers with prepaid medical care.

· JACK DEURLOO ·

His formula was simple: "Find a need and fill it." He was an old-fashioned self-made man. He spoke slowly and deliberately, but moved and though fast. He was fond of homely aphorisms. "There's only one time to do anything," he would say, "and that's today".

Mission Impossible

Henry never knows what he can't do, a rival said – and it seemed to be true.

When he won the seven million dollar contract to supply cement for the huge Shasta Dam in California, he didn't even have a cement plant. But in seven months he built the biggest plant in the world. When he got his first ship-building contract in World War II, he had no shipyards and had never built a ship. At the time, the job was done by hand, patiently and piece by piece, taking months or even years. This was too slow for Henry. Why not prefabricate sections, then assemble them on the way? Told that it was impossible, he built his own shipyards, got on with the job – and revolutionized shipbuilding.

Henry soon had 200,000 workers toiling in seven shipyards along the Pacific Coast. His time for building a Liberty ship fell from an average of 253 day to 26. One Kaiser yard built a ship in 4 days, 15 hours, 26 minutes – from keel-laying to launching!

I saw Henry often when he came to New York. He wore a watch on each wrist – one on California time, where his headquarters were, the other on local time. He traveled about 75,000 miles a year in those days, and his phone bill ran about $300,000 annually. Even when he went out to dinner, he often had a phone plugged in to cal one of his shipyards – sometimes all of them at once in a conference call. His key aides got used to being awaken at 3 or 4 am by Henry's cheerful voice announcing, "I just had an idea. Maybe it's crazy but....."

A Mink for Mama

Away from his work, Henry was a simple, easygoing man. One of his few pleasures was dining at a good restaurant with his wife Bess, whom he called "Mama". The only extravagance I ever saw him indulge in was when he bought Bell a mink coat. I went with them to Bergdorf Goodman's, where Mrs. Kaiser selected skins for the coat. And then Henry did a thing unheard of in the mink-coat business. "I'd like it delivered by next Monday," he said.

"But that's not enough time," the salesman protested.

"Not enough time!" Kaiser exclaimed. "If I can build two Liberty ships in a week, you can make one mink coat," and they did.

To Henry there was really no such thing as work. "It's all occupation," he said. And Henry had kept occupied from the time he was in knee pants.

The son of German immigrants, he was born in Sprout Brook, N.Y., in 1882, one of four children. He left school at 13 to help support his family. A few years later he got a job selling photographic supplies in upstate New York. He met a lake Placid photo-shop owner and told him: "I think I can double your sales. I'll work for a year without salary; but if I do double your business, I want to become a partner." The owner agreed. Young Kaiser *trebled* the business and, within another year, he bought out his partner. He was then 23.

Restless, Kaiser moved to Florida, where he opened photo shops in several cities. Then he set out for Spokane, Washington, where he tried the sand and gravel business. In 1914 he borrowed money to buy some second-hand concrete mixers, and went into the construction business.

Happy Elephant

From the outset Kaiser showed a knack for overcoming problems. Building a highway near Seattle, he needed water but couldn't afford gasoline for a pump to bring it from a nearby river. So he improvised. He fitted a barge with a paddlewheel from a riverboat and used the rotating wheel to power his pump.

For the next dozen years Kaiser built roads all over the northwest. He was buff, hard-driving, but his crews liked him. "Henry is like a happy elephant," an associate said. "He smiles and leans against you. After a while you know there's nothing left to do but move in the direction he's pushing."

In the late 1920's Kaiser was building roads in Cuba when he heard of plans to build the Hoover Dam on the Colorado River – a project of gigantic proportions. "I lay awake nights in my sweltering tent and think about it," he later recalled. "I know it was too big for me, yet I figured there must be *some* way to get in on it."

Finally he hit on an idea: Why not get a group of big contractors to pool their resources? A half dozen of them agreed and formed Six Companies Inc., with Kaiser as chairman of the executive committee. They landed the contract, and finished the 726 foot high dam in two years ahead of schedule. Later Kaiser helped build the Bonneville and Grand Coulee dams on the Columbia River, both completed well ahead of the target date.

New Dealings

He tore into any project with vigour. Dealing with Washington during the war, Henry descended with all the push of a bulldozer. He was a desk-pounder, and arm-waver, a lapel-grabber. Understandably, he ruffled some feathers but, before long, Presidential adviser Thomas Corcoran was calling Kaiser "one of the great natural resources of a nation at war."

A covey of bright young men fielded the orders, ideas and exhortations that he spouted as he charged along, and translated them into action. He never hesitated to admit ignorance. "I make progress by having people around me who are smarter than I am and listening to them," he once told me. "And I assume that everyone is smarter about something than I am."

Four-Wheel Flop

At the end of the war, Kaiser Shipyards were turning out one Liberty ship a day and one aircraft carrier a week. Many doubted that he could convert his huge war oriented empire to peacetime production.

Kaiser's first postwar undertaking was a fiasco. He teamed up with veteran automobile man Joseph W. Frazer to form the Kaiser-Fraser automobile company. They leased the huge Willow Run plant outside Detroit and began turning out a Kaiser, a Frazer and a compact Henry J. And for the first time in his life, Kaiser came a cropper. His company lost more than $100 million dollars in the ill starred venture.

But Henry seemed to thrive on trouble. When I asked him what he planned to do next, he said, "Well, I leased an aluminum plant for the auto company, so now I'm in the aluminum business. And I built a steel plant for the shipyards, so I'm in the steel business. Don't worry about me."

Henry went into these new enterprises with his usual drive. As always, he was scornful of obstacles. When he built a new aluminum plant in New Orleans, Charles E. Wilson, head of the office of Defence Mobilization, asked him for a certain production potential. "Sure, we can produce that much," Kaiser said.

"In fact, would you like us to double that figure?" One of his aides tugged at Henry's arm and whispered,

"Take it easy, H.J., Remember, Rome wasn't built in a day.

"I wouldn't know about that," Kaiser grunted. "I wasn't working on that job."

Today, Kaiser Aluminum is the world's fourth largest aluminum company, and Kaiser Steel the ninth largest U.S. steel company. Henry also went right on building dame, in Greece, Australia, Ghana and Venezuela, automobile industries in Argentina and Brazil, and the largest aluminum smelter in Africa. He also became interested in health care, and began to build the network of self-sustaining Kaiser hospitals and clinics that now provide medical care in the American West. "The thing I would like to be remembered for is the hospitals," he said to me. "They make me feel as if I had fulfilled a need."

Operation Retirement

At the age of 73, Henry turned over active direction of his far-flung enterprises to his son Edgar and went to Hawaii for a vacation. Of course, he couldn't rest. I got a card from him telling me of his plans for a hotel called the Hawaiian Village. And that was only the start. His building eventually grew into a 6,000 acre, $350 million real estate development, including a resort and a hospital.

When my wife and I visited him shortly before his death last August, he showed us around proudly. All his equipment, from bulldozers and dredges to jeeps and catamarans, was in his favourite color – bright pink. He was over 80 but having the time of his life. Up every morning at 5 o'clock, he would switch on both television and radio to hear the news on his stations while he ate a hearty breakfast. Then he was off and running to inspect the progress of his huge development being built on former salt marshes and volcanic slopes at the Eastern end of Oahu Island.

It was in Hawaii that I saw him last. We were sitting on his lawn looking out over the pacific under a starry sky. Henry was talking about one of his favourite subjects, "people building" as he called it. "You find your key men by piling work on them. They say, "Sure you can." Pretty soon they are doing more that they knew they could, and you have an organization that can really get things done."

Proud of his ability to get people to work together, he couldn't tolerate "yes-men." "I've got one employee who in 50 years has never agreed with me on anything," he said. "He's invaluable."

Suddenly, he changed the subject, pointed to some ornamental crystal balls he had suspended in big-looped nets, from the side of his house. "I wove those nets myself," he said proudly. "The first loop took me three minutes. Then I got it down to two loops in three minutes. Finally I could do those loops in one minute each."

The spirit was Henry J. Kaiser's secret for doing the impossible.

· CHAPTER 8 ·

What Are You Afraid Of?

Linda, 25, is unable to enter elevators without feeling panic. Robert, 57, worries almost constantly about his approaching retirement. Phyllis, 15, awaits the arrival of her date; her knees feel shaky, her stomach is upset.

At all ages, fear presents a problem to almost everyone. "We are largely the playthings for our fears," wrote British author Horace Walpole many years ago. "To one, fear of the dark; to another, of physical pain; to a third, of public ridicule; to a forth, of poverty; to a fifth, of loneliness – for all of us our particular creature waits in ambush."

Fear if often a most useful emotion. When you become frightened, many physical changes occur within your body. Your heartbeat and responses quicken; your pupils dilate and admit more light. Large quantities of energy-producing adrenalin are poured into your bloodstream; confronted with a fire or an impending accident, fear can fuel life-saving flight. Similarly, when the danger is psychological, rather than physical, fear can force you to take self-protective measures. It is only within fear is disproportionate to the danger at hand that it becomes a problem.

Some people are simply more susceptible to fear than others. A visit to the newborn nursery of any large hospital will demonstrate that, from the moment of birth, a few fortunate infants respond calmly to sudden fear-producing situations such as a loudly slammed door. Yet a neighbour in the next crib may cry out with profound fright. From birth, he/she is more prone to learn fearful responses because he/she has *inherited* a tendency to be more sensitive.

Further, psychologists know that our early experiences and relationships strongly shape and determine our later fears. A young man named Bill, for example, grew up with a father who regarded each adversity as a temporary obstacle to be overcome. Using his father as a model, Bill came to welcome adventure and to trust in his own ability to solve problems.

Phil's dad, however continually tried to protect himself and his family. Afraid to risk the insecurity of a job change, he remained unhappily in one position. He avoided long vacations because "the car might break down." Growing up in such a home, Phil naturally learned to become fearful.

Perhaps the most destructive form of fear is the chronic, gnawing pain of anxiety, which haunts the lives of so many people. Anxiety is particularly difficult to bear because it usually lacks a specific focus.

Fortunately, even people who are frequently beset by unwarranted fears and anxieties can take steps to reduce most of them to tolerable size. Here are some suggestions:

1. *Respect your body.* Every person suffering from excessive fear should have a thorough physical examination. You cannot feel free from fear if you are malnourished, ill or tired. I recall one woman, initially complaining of continual fear, who was found to have the beginnings of hypoglycaemia, a low blood-sugar condition. If, however, examination reveals no physical cause for your fear, stop blaming

you body and investigate your conflicts of your faulty learnings.

2. *Share your feelings.* Fears thrive on secrecy and a sense of being "very special". In 1968, Prof. Irving Janis, a psychologist at Yale University, studied a group of surgical patients. Some worried out loud before surgery; others expressed little apprehension, indeed seemed to exhibit confidence. Curiously, the first group experienced fewer postoperative complications and had an easier convalescence than those stoic patients who felt they had to bear their fears by themselves.

The best people for you to talk to about a fear are those directly involved in your worries. If you can reveal your feelings to them without blaming them for your fear, you have taken an important step. If you cannot, try turning to a trusted friend, religious counsellor or teacher.

3. Accept brief periods of fear. Fearful concern is the natural companion to most major changes in our lives. Recently, a patient came to me who had moved three times in the past four years. I soon realized that she was reacting to the natural anxieties that result from so much intensive change. When she began to accept her fears as natural, she gained control.

4. *Learn to love in the present.* If you'll honestly examine your worst fears, you'll almost invariably find them to be of the "what would happen if" variety. Many are born of imaginings that simply aren't true. They constitute what I call the "suppose" syndrome –

suppose I fail a test, fall ill, lose my friends, make a poor impression, etc.

5. *Listen to what you tell yourself.* People often worsen their fears by seeing situations as catastrophic. What you tell yourself about a situation is usually the way that you will begin to respond to that situation. If, for example, your car breaks down, the healthy reaction is, "well, it's an inconvenience, but scarcely a tragedy." If, however, you choose to tell yourself such things as, "It always happens to me – I'm a born loser," you're likely to lead yourself into self-pity and chronic anxiety.

6. *Stop being a perfectionist.* If you truly want to do a *good* job, you will usually succeed. If you want to do a perfect job, however, you may well be defeated before you start. A friend of mine had whipped herself into a frenzy of worry over giving a dinner party for some of her husband's business associates. As I listened to her, I sensed that her true fear did not arise from her plans to give a simple dinner party; actually, she wanted to outdo all of the dinner parties that she had attended that year. By wanting everything to be perfect, she placed an unnecessary strain on herself.

7. *Learn to relax.* A person cannot be relaxed and frightened at the same time. But most fearful people doubt that they can ever relax. When I suggested relaxation exercises to one frightened, tense man, he said, "If I could relax, I wouldn't be in a psychologist's office." I had to agree, but relaxation is a skill which can be learned – for example, by sitting down in a comfortable chair, breathing in slowly, then gradually exhaling. By

gaining control of your breathing you can often lesson the symptoms of fear.

For those who are interested in learning about relaxation, many local evening schools, YMCAs and YWCAs have begun to offer courses in yoga and in meditation.

8. *Look for a meaning for your life.* Without s sense of meaning, people become cynical, then scared. Religious faith is a fortress for many in times of stress. So is serving the needs of others. An elderly man I know, fretful over his health, learned about the "foster grandparent" plan in his city. As he began to devote hours to his foster grandchild, he had less time to dwell on his own fears. In working with this underprivileged boy, he found the meaning for his life.

Perhaps that is the best wisdom of all. By giving of yourself, you often lose your fears.

· CHAPTER 9 ·

Eight Steps to a New Life

Forty years of listening to troubled people has made me familiar, I think, with just about every human problem under the sun. But there's one so prevalent that I consider it the basic human sickness. It's the problem of the person who is living far below his/her potential and knows it; who is deeply unhappy, but can't seem to do anything about it.

Usually, from where the counsellor sits, the person's difficulties don't seem so overwhelming – but the sufferer is convinced he/she can't cope with them. Although he/she seems to have normal intelligence, adequate education and all the necessary attributes for successful living, he/she can't summon them to his/her aid. Their life is blurred, out of focus, without power or purpose.

Always, you find three deadly characteristics in such people: inertia, self-doubt and aimlessness. One autumn day, walking alone around our local golf course (I was hoping to share some lecture ideas); I came upon a young man raking leaves off a green. I knew him slightly and I asked how things were going.

He shrugged, "as you can see", he said, "I'm not getting anywhere."

"Where do you want to get," I asked.

He looked at me glumly, "I don't really know," he said.

"What do you do best?" I asked. He shook his head. "I'm not sure that I'm much good at anything."

"Well, what gives out the most satisfaction?"

He frowned. "No special things."

"Look," I said, "I've asked you three of the most important questions anyone can be asked, and I had three completely fuzzy answers. When you go home tonight, I want you to sit down with paper and pencil, and don't get up until you've answered my questions. Then let's meet here tomorrow at this time, and we'll take it from there."

Somewhat hesitantly, he agreed. When we met the next day, he told me that he liked to work with his hands, not his head: that he thought he might have some mechanical ability; and that what he wanted most in life was some sense of purpose or direction. Shortly thereafter, he got a job in a roofing-materials factory. Did he become president of the company? No, but today he is a foreman, living a happy and productive life. All he needed was a push to stop leading an unfocused life.

I meet people like that young man so frequently that I have developed a set of guidelines to help anyone, young or old, who feels the need to bring himself into sharper focus. There are eight points in all, and they add up to quite a stiff course in self-discipline. But anyone who makes a sustained effort to apply them will become a happier, more forceful, more effective person.

1. *Pinpoint your primary goal in life.* It's not enough to say, "I want to be happy" or "I want to make money" or "I want to be a better person." You must determine exactly what you want, and when. You need to say, "I intend to be a registered nurse in three years," or sales manager of this company, or editor of this newspaper, or buyer for that store, in four, five or six years.

2. *Use Imagination to fan desire.* There's no use pinpointing a goal in life unless you want it enormously. Daydreams and wishful wishes are not enough; there must be intense, burning desire. Nobody can put this hunger into you; you have to develop it yourself by constant, vivid imagining of the benefits that achieving your goal will bring. Ask anyone who has achieved outstanding success in any field. He will tell you that clarity of purpose and intensity of desire are the chief ingredients of the magic formula. Unless you care, you won't get there.

3. *Expect to pay for what you get.* If you set a high goal, you will have to pay a high price. You have to work, take chances, make sacrifices, and endure setbacks. You won't be able to afford the luxury of laziness or the delights of frequent distraction. When setting your goal, remember that unless you're willing to pay the price you're wasting your time.

4. *Send the right signals to your unconscious mind.* This is crucial. The unconscious is a great dynamo. But it is also a computer that has to be properly programmed. If fear thoughts, worry thoughts, failure thoughts are constantly channelled into the unconscious, nothing very constructive is going to be sent back. But if a clear, purposeful goal is steadfastly held in the conscious mind, the unconscious will eventually accept it and begin to supply the conscious mind with plans, ideas, insights, and the energies necessary to achieve that goal.

5. *Be willing to fail – temporarily.* A man who made a long-term study of highly successful men in various fields told me that he noted they had only one trait in common; persistence. They kept picking themselves

up and returning to the fight long after most men or women would have given up.

In a lecture not long ago, I condensed the life history of such a man. This man failed in business in '31. He was defeated for the State Legislature in '32. He failed again in business in '34. He had a nervous breakdown in '41. He hoped to receive his party's nomination for Congress but didn't, in '43. He ran for Senate and lost in '55. He was defeated again for the Senate in '58. A hopeless loser, some people said. But Abraham Lincoln was elected President in 1860. He knew how to accept defeat – temporarily.

6. *Believe in the power of thought to change things.* It's very hard for most people to realize that the most powerful force in the world is an idea that has taken root in a human mind. But it is.

Not long ago in Australia, I met a remarkable man named Bert Walton. He told me that he had started out in life by failing at one school after another, then at one job after another. He was working for the Australian division of an American corporation – and going downhill at that – when a man came out from the parent company to talk to Australian employees. One sentence in the man's talk struck Walton with enormous impact: *You can – if you think you can.*

"I suddenly realized," Walton told me, "that the reason I was a failure was my habit of thinking of myself as a failure. The concept created the condition – not the other way around. So I decided to change the concept. I said to myself: 'I think I can become manager of this company for New South Wales. In fact, I think I can become manager for the whole of Australia.' And eventually that happened too. I'm a very ordinary man, but I got hold of one extraordinary idea, and hung on."

What happened to that man? The idea, like a burning glass, focused the rays of his personality on a definite goal with such intensity that hitherto inert elements burst into flame. The idea is not a new one. The bible says "If ye have faith, nothing shall be impossible unto you." A staggering promise, certainly, but profoundly true.

7. *Never build a case against yourself.* Just last week, a man came up to me and asked if we could talk. He had a stooped, dejected look. And he sounded defeated. "I'm a salesman," he said. "I make a living at it, but my work is of no importance. I'm depressed and miserable most of the time. Can you help me?"

"No", I said. "I can't crawl into your head and rearrange the machinery. But perhaps I can tell you how to help yourself.

In the first place, stop cringing. Stand up straight. Next, stop running down your profession. In our society, salesmen are the ball bearings on which industry moves; without them, the economy would grind to a halt. Finally, why don't you stop looking at yourself from a worm's viewpoint and look at yourself from God's? You are His child. If you are important to Him – and you are – what gives you the right to go around proclaiming your unimportance?"

We talked a bit more; then he thanked me, and went away looking thoughtful. I hope he had learned, or

75

begun to learn, the importance of not building a case against himself.

8. *Stop short-circuiting yourself with alibis.* Unfocused people do this constantly. They say, "The timing is wrong" or "I'm not really qualified." They play the if-only game: "If only I had more money, or more education ... if only I weren't so tied down..." the alibis go on and on, and they just reinforce the three deadly characteristics − inertia, self-doubt, aimlessness. To become a focused person you have to control self-limiting thoughts. "I don't believe in circumstances." George Bernard Shaw once said. "The people who get on in this world are the people who look for the circumstances they want, and if they can't find them, they make them."

Plato once said that the unexamined life isn't worth living. The statement is as true today as it was 23 centuries ago. So, examine your life. If it is out of focus, make up your mind to get it into focus. And start today.

CHAPTER 10

The Growth of Confidence

After you know what you want, and you are definite about it, and after you have put all fears behind you, then you will set up into a new phase of life. A phase that has much to do with your own development, a phase that will do much to carry you forward to your Power-aim.

You will feel a confidence surging within you. You will feel a glorious Power within you. You will have supreme faith in yourself.

Knowing that you have complete control of your thinking, you will recognize the Power that is to give your self-confidence a solid foundation.

You are an individual. Your thinking is straight and true. You are honest in your self-analysis. You are consciously correcting your faults. You have learned to bear with other people. You are no longer lonesome and alone. Your thoughts are with you at all times. They are helping you in every step you take along your path. You no longer fear the truth. You understand that the truth is your rightful heritage. The truth has now become an integral part of your daily life. You are the truth and the truth is you. You can now face the world, knowing that you fear no man.

From now on, you will be the pure manifestation of your thoughts. You will be what you think you are. You will think health and you will be healthy. You will think beauty and you will be beautiful. You will think of the Master's unlimited supply and it will be yours to use wisely. You will think love to all the world and love will come into your life. You will, at all times, be the result of your thinking.

In your daily work, in your contacts with others, in your own silent sessions with the Master, you will find yourself growing to a new stature.

The problems that have heretofore seemed insurmountable will have dissolved. They will cease to exist. Your thinking and the divine truth will be your constant protection.

You will be like a new-born child, learning to walk, learning to walk your own way alone, unafraid, confident.

People will appear before you in their true proportions and their honest importance. Those, whom you deemed great, will now assume their human stature with all their human weaknesses and frailties clear to your eye. Those who seemed to fill you with fear and dread will no longer cause you to tremble.

The liar, the fraud and the cheat will not be able to fool you for truth being on your side; will protect you by revealing itself to you. The thief can take nothing from you for your treasure will be in your confidence, in your faith in yourself.

The future will have no terrors for you, for now you know that the future can only bring you greater confidence, greater power, greater understanding.

Now you will stand on your own feet. You will look to no one but the Master for help. You will know that your help comes from within. It will come from the power that you have created within yourself.

Tomorrow will no longer be a day to look forward to with dread and fear. You will look to all your tomorrows with confidence. Tomorrow will mean another opportunity for you to exercise your new strength.

Yesterday will be a book that you will study in order to find new ways to improve yourself.

Today will be yours forever. To do with as you know is right.

Each morning and each evening, as you appear before yourself, in the Power building sessions of the silence, you will say over and over again, until it is a part of your being:

I AM THE PERFECT CHILD OF THE MASTER. I LIVE PERFECTION. I THINK PERFECTION. I AM PREFECTION. EACH NEW DAY, EACH NEW HOUR OFFERS ME NEW OPPORTUNITIES FOR THE PERFECT EXPRESSION OF MY PERFECTION.

Repeat this over and over. You will find the words guiding you to the perfect state that is your Power-aim.

Once your confidence is firmly rooted in the ground that you have so faithfully cultivated, you will be ready to go onto the next step.

Now, your will takes over, and you begin to feel and experience the fruits of your earlier application. Instead of playing a passive role, your will takes an active part in all the things you do. You call on your WILL on all occasions and your will responds. You climb to new heights. New vistas unfold themselves before your eager eyes. A new world opens up to you, the world of will.

I have found that most of the people who live on this earth, aspire to something or other at various times in their lives. This goal may be money, power, position, influence, health or any of the ends towards which man aspires. Yet, despite their very best intentions, they never seem to attain their desires. Why? There is but one answer. These people are not sufficiently definite about their goal, if they have a goal at all. They do not live their aspirations twenty-four hours a day. There are far too many unconnected interests that come between them and their Power-aim.

They are very much like the child in front of a Christmas tree. There are so many packages; so many glittering trinkets hanging from the tree, the youngster cannot concentrate his interest on any one thing.

These people are like the man who starved in the midst of plenty because he could not make up his mind which of the tempting morsels he should eat.

So you, who cannot bring yourself to that state where you can keep your eyes and your mind in one direction long enough to make that direction yours, you will find that your goal, your aspiration, your Power-aim will escape you. It will slip though your finders like sand.

To wish for something is not enough. To feel that you should have what you are after is not enough. To hope for your goal is not enough. To dream of your Power-aim is not enough. YOU MUST WILL IT – actively – at all times.

When your will takes over, when it takes complete charge of your every action, when it assumes complete control of your every thought, then, and not until then, will you be on the road to your goal.

Your will can exert a power greater than any, for the work of the day that is before you.

Your faith can move mountains. Will thinks with all the will at your command. A thing is so, simply because you will it. Nothing can stand in the way of your will if you know how to control it.

You can have an unlimited supply. You can have an unending supply. A supply that is only limited by your own willingness to admit that there is a limited supply. If you know and feel and understand that this unlimited Power that comes from within can take you wherever you will. You can do whatever you will. You can attain whatever you will.

This silence, where you store up your supply of will, must never be negative. It must not be a resting period. It must not be a period of day-dreaming, of idle wishing, it must be positive, dynamic, and alive.

You must make it a Positive Period

You must, by the exercise of your self-control, by your ability to concentrate, by your ability to recognize the Word when it comes to you, make of this regular communication with your inner self and with the Master, a period in which you make your plans to conquer your world.

Undirected will takes the line of least resistance. It takes the easy way. Just as a brook winds its way around boulders and through gullies, your undirected will finds it much easier to go around obstacles than it would be to overcome them.

Remember, a dead fish floats with the current. It takes a live one to swim against the tide. Build up your will until you reach that stage in life when each new obstacle is welcomes as an opportunity to exercise your new found Power. Then, when you have yourself well in hand, when you know where you are going, when you begin to recognize the new found strength that stems from within you, when your eye and your mind and your heart are centred on the goal that is yours, then...you are ready for the next step.

Like a child learning to walk along, you step out, cautiously at first, to test the strength and extent of your new-found Power. As you discover that you can now do some of the things you previously had merely hoped to do, you experience the beginnings of courage.

Now, you are having your first demonstration of your new-found Power.

The Process of Getting Ahead Sooner

This is not the end. It's but the beginning. You still have quite a distance to go. Now, you build your goal carefully, stone on stone, you become the architect of your own destiny, you draw the plans of your Power-aim with all its' details.

You already built the foundations in your earlier exercises. Now, you must be ready to go ahead. To stand still is to go back.

In life nothing stands still. It either moves forward or moves backward. With your goal before you, you must move ahead, towards it. Any neglect, delay or temporary halt is a backward step.

Plan your edifice with your ideals. Make your will the corner-stone of your building, for with the true exercise of your will, you become the embodiment of your ideals.

Your thoughts should be high; as high as you can aspire. You must, at all times, remember that you can be what you think you are. The higher your thoughts, your ideals, your power-aim, the higher will be the goal you will finally reach.

Fresh from a session with your Master in the silence, you will find yourself looking upon the world with a new-found courage. You look upon the world that meets you with different eyes, with deeper understanding. You know where you are going. The aimless intentions of the rest of the world are apparent to you and you avoid them. You are now an individual with a definite aim. You have an appointment with destiny. You are now on your way to your power-aim.

You feel the new born strength of your intentions. You learn the most important lesson that life has to teach you. You learn that this tremendous power-energy that is now a part of everything you feel, think, or do, is something that works through you. You are the medium through which it expresses itself.

Learn to repeat the Litany of your Faith

You repeat this over and over again, until the true meanings of the words are revealed to you. They are revealed to you not in the static sense, as words along, but, in their active sense of power working through you.

Words have a way of working for you. Your faith and your belief give them an intensity that is overwhelming. They are at once a challenge and an obligation, a challenge to attain and the obligation to be true to yourself, your thinking and your faith.

Tomorrow no longer holds terrors for you. Your work, be it what it may, takes on a new proportion, assumes a new importance. Heretofore, it was merely a means to an end. It meant food, clothing and shelter. Now, it is something quite different. It is no longer a necessary social obligation alone.

Your work becomes an opportunity to serve, an opportunity to help those around you, an opportunity for you to grow in importance, in understanding and in accomplishment.

You are above jealousy and envy, for now you realize that these are the emotions that would hold you back. They would keep you from your power-aim. They are typical fear manifestations that you have learned to overcome in the early stages of your education.

The spite or envy of others can no longer harm you. You are impervious to all their barbs. You rise above the petty people and events. You are now the master of your own intentions. You are not ruler of your own thoughts. You are now the dictator of your own actions.

Your mind takes on new power. It sees through the shams of life. It intuitively understands and anticipates the intentions of others. You are far beyond the heavy load of circumstances. You now create your own circumstances. You have risen above the crowd. All because you have learned the real meaning of the words you say. Because of your understanding, because you have learned how to accept this help that is always ready for you, because they are no longer mere words, but your testament of faith. Each time you repeat them, you strengthen your faith in your approach to your power-aim.

I, of Myself, do Nothing. The Power within Me Does all Things.

By this time, if you have been continuing your exercises in the silence, with fidelity, you should be able to achieve demonstrations of your own.

You are no longer wishing, hoping or dreaming of everything that comes into the mind. You are definitely concentrating all your WILL on the one goal that you have already so carefully selected.

You will find that your daily work, if you conduct it with sincerity, will be another way of reaching upwards and onwards toward your power-aim.

A great many people feel that unless their work has some glamour or some seemingly interesting feature, it is just something that takes up the time of the day. That it is merely a means of obtaining the necessities of life. They do just what is expected of them or as little as they possibly can without being discharged from their position. They feel that they are fooling the boss. They are not doing all the things that he expects them to do. They are fools. They believe that they are cleverer than others.

Unfortunately, these people are merely fooling themselves. They are losing their greatest opportunity to practice for the days when their work will be entirely the work of their own power-aim.

You should bear in mind every job you do, no matter how small or mental it may be, is always another test, another trail and another opportunity to grow and become proficient in the exercise of your own will.

You, like many others, may not feel that your superior is treating you with the consideration you deserve. You may feel that she/he is favouring others, that he/she does not recognize your importance, your seriousness, our application or your efforts.

All these occasions are just additional opportunities for you, opportunities to show yourself that you can do what is right, that you can do as much as is required of you, and that you can do it intelligently. You don't have to try to prove it to your superior. Just prove it to yourself. Remember that you are the most important person in our own life. You are the one that must be satisfied with our own progress. You are the boss at all times. You are the person who sets the tune.

Some of your short sighted fellow workers may try to undermine you. They may circulate false stories about you. They may try to lower you in the eyes of your superiors. Pay no heed to them. They cannot harm you. You are above then, for your protection is much stronger than the will of others. You are divinely protected, for your store of faith, built up during your sessions in the silent is stronger than any steel armour that you can wear.

These people do themselves far more harm than they can ever do to you. Their envy, their jealousy, their spite, merely builds up their own inferiority. They are merely adding to their store of fear.

A person is merely the extension of his thoughts. You are what you think. If you think power at all times, you will exert power. If you think hate, you will merely build up your own store of hate. Be one who, at all times, radiates love, friendship, confidence and helpfulness.

You will soon impress those who come in contact with you. You will know how to use the power of your thoughts. People around you will be quick to sense the beauty and the peace that constantly surround you.

Think back to the days when you disliked people. The more you disliked, the more reason there was to dislike them and others. Therefore, keep your thoughts clean of all petty things. Do not fill your mind and your thinking with disagreeable thoughts. They multiply so quickly that you will soon find yourself overwhelmed by thoughts that will hold you back from the attainment of your power-aim.

They will hesitate before they try to undermine you, for they will soon realize that they cannot harm you, that you are above all the petty thoughts and deeds that are a part of their lives.

In this way, you will become a leader, one who will inspire others, one who will show the way to the weaklings.

The person who is always looking for a fight or an argument is not a person of power. He is the embodiment of weakness. His/her belligerence is the only means that he/she has to prove to himself/herself that he/she is not a coward or a fool. The great tragedy of his/her life comes when he/she meets someone who is either stronger or can speak louder. His is a false strength, and a false confidence. The strength which is built on the solid foundation of your perfect understanding of your power can never be destroyed or weakened.

Your confidence in yourself has the strength of a stone wall that cannot be battered down. For you, understanding the sources of your strength can keep renewing it from time to time. You can always, at any time, at any place and under any circumstances, call upon the source of your power and add to the directness and the definiteness of your aim.

This is the power that can never be shaken. This is the glory that can never be dimmed.

With this power at your command, you can stand on your feet. You can look into the eyes of the world unafraid. You can do the things that man had never done before.

The affirmation that you use at this stage of your progress is a simple one, one that embodies the story of your growth, the heart of your message and the soul of your power.

The Power of the Master, manifested through me, gives me my share of life's abundance.

With this step, you come to the stage in your progress where your will is constantly directing you in all the things you undertake. With your newly developed sense of understanding, you know that you are being divinely guided.

Each morning, as you sit in the silence, with the master, you discover that your day's instructions are being made understandable to you. This may sound strange to you on the first reading, but it is so.

In the silence, your mind being at rest, your thoughts concentrated on your regular meetings with the Master, you will find thoughts coming and going through your mind. Let them come and go. That is the way to clear your mind for the real message.

Your self-training will have taught you to recognize thoughts that come direct from your power-source and separate them from those thoughts wish-borne.

Ideas will crystallize in your consciousness. You will get what many people call "hunches". These so-called hunches are very often messages, instructions that you must follow.

In the silence, the things that you had hitherto never understood will make themselves clear to you. You will see and understand the true reasons for things, events and thoughts. You will begin to understand the manner in which the Master works out your destiny in His own way.

You are no longer in the dark, but, in life's most revealing and brightest light. You are the centre of the universe. Into you now pours the power to continue onward and upward, and in turn, from you will radiate all your good thoughts for others, all your good intentions, all the concentrated glory for your Master-source.

The Process of Getting Ahead Sooner

The thoughts that come to you in the silence are the messages that are meant exclusively for you and for no other. They are the guide-posts that will show you the way ahead. They are the instructions that the master-mind has created and issued just for you. You reach out for these messages and take them to yourself. They are your way.

Don't let them pass unnoticed. Make it your business to understand them clearly. You will be able to recognize how they fit into the pattern of your individual power-aim. You will see the reason for them.

You reach out and take them to you. You reach out and follow these instructions. You reach out and encompass in your embrace, the will of the Master.

By following your instructions, you will notice how such further ahead you go, how much faster you progress, and how much greater becomes your strength.

The unknowing around you, will call your advancement and your accomplishments a miracle. You, knowing and understanding from where it comes, will be glad to give it its correct name, which is progress.

Your progress will depend on how well you follow your instructions, how sincere you are in the application of the basic laws and how seriously you apply your concentrated will on the attainment of your goal.

Keep your work to yourself. Don't discuss it with others. Discussing it with others is a sign of your lack of faith in yourself. It is a sign of weakness. It is a sign that you are seeking commendation from those whom you have tried to impress with your ambition. It's a sign of vanity.

Your work, your ambitions, your power-aim is a matter that concerns but you and the Master. Go to Him with your problems. Go to Him with your questions. Then, you are assured that they will be answered quickly and correctly.

Do not rely on mere man's judgment when you have the judgment of the all wise at your command. The more often you call on the master for help and advice, the more you will be able to stand on your own feet and the greater will be your power. For the guiding spirit of the will within you becomes more potent with use.

The more you use your will, the stronger it becomes.

You will find that the more you reach out for, the more you will accomplish. Your accomplishments will be limited only by your will to attain.

Do not limit yourself. Do not draw an imaginary line and say to yourself: "So far, will I go and no further". Do not even think the words, for the very thought itself will limit your power of accomplishment. Realize that there is no limit to your own strength when it is coupled with the strength of the Master's. There can be no limit to your power when it is one with the power-source.

No outside influence can limit you. Limitation can only come from within; you are the only person who can defeat your own aims.

You can, therefore, see the importance of your self-confidence, the necessity of your self-development and the need for your complete and undivided faith.

Always be ready to meet your problems face to face, with the Master at your side and call upon Him at all times for your guidance, support and strength.

Keep on repeating the words endlessly and meaningfully:

I, of Myself, do Nothing. The Power within Me Does all Things.

CHAPTER 11

The Monarch Butterfly

There are all kinds of butterflies in the Peterborough area, where I live. There are as many different butterflies as there are birds in the world and we have them all. It is claimed that there are about 65 different butterflies in this area. As you know, they all have beautiful colors and names, but I like the talk about the Monarch butterfly. They have distinctly gorgeous colors. Do you know that when the cold weather approaches, they all fly to the south to Mexico and Brazil. Do you realize that their brain is as small as a pinhead and their wings are thinner than a tissue paper? Yet, they make it all the way there, thousands of miles away. People claim that they go back to the same area each year and some of them (some claim) go back to the same tree as their ancestors. They fly by instinct alone.

These little creatures go for thousands of miles and we, with all our senses can't find out cell phones!

Then there is the squirrel, who gathers nuts and food in the fall for the winter, even the young ones that were born last spring gather nuts and food, and they don't even know what winter is all about!

Why is it that you or I, with a "working" brain cannot get out of life, what Mother Nature has given us? All the power, al the intellect, all the strength as a human being to think and make something good in this life we have. Why do we keep complaining about big and small problems? Stop complaining, "suck it up", and go on with your life. Take off those cement shoes you're wearing and close the door on the negative stuff. Put a new tape in that brain of yours with positive ideas and learn to grow up and become that man or woman you can be. Arouse the sleeping greatness within you. Set aside your fears, worries, doubts, boredom and your "stinking negative thinking to eliminate and avoid the hardening of your attitude".

You have to change your thought pattern. You have to recognize opportunities, set goals, use your mind, and have personal growth and self control. Use your imagination; use the science I told you about.

The "science" is the ABC of getting what you want through repeating the science so your subconscious mind will take over and things will change in our life.

When a Monarch butterfly can fly miles and miles on instinct, so you too have the power to change circumstances around you.

How to Get the BEST Out of Life

How many of us feel stuck because we keep looking for answers in the wrong place? We keep searching in the same spot because it's familiar to us, even though it doesn't bring us happiness. We refuse to explore new areas that appear unfamiliar or threatening even when they might lead us out of our predicament. We keep trying to solve our problems in the same old ways that we already know do not work. We keep going back to the same people for the same rejections and we cling to the past.

This writing gives you positive, healthy messages we send to ourselves – helps – us to overcome roadblocks and find new paths. They show us how to let go of the past and open ourselves to the present.

Reflect on each message and silently apply them to your life. You will become actively involved in your own healing process as you write your own healing of the mind and body process. We get the best out of life from moving forward, not moving backward or standing still. Fear of the unfamiliar stunts our growth. The answers come when we search unfamiliar areas, by trying something new and different, by putting ourselves out these to take risks. These affirming messages will give you the empowerment you've been looking for.

Finding What You Want

Whatever we look for, we will discover. Whatever we expect usually comes through for us. As the saying goes, "seek and you shall find". We set our sights in a certain direction and ultimately see whatever we expect to see. This seems like a very simple idea but one that is powerful and far reaching.

When we look for miser, we will find it. When we look for joy, we will find joy. When we look for prosperity, we will find prosperity. When we look for pain and rejection, we will find them also.

We can put simple principles into everyday use. We create our experiences of life in the things we find and hold on to. Whatever we look for is waiting for us.

The Eliminating Of Our Wants

Our mind desires certain things in life and as one want is satisfied, another one appears. The desire for a drink, a piece of pizza, a new wardrobe, a car, a beautiful house, another relationship, etc. Wanting is an ongoing cycle that never stops. Our wants are never satisfied. As long as we stay focused on wanting, we will always feel that our lives are lacking. We can eliminate our wants by giving ourselves spiritual nourishment. We become fulfilled by turning inward to the heart and filling it with love, compassion, acceptance and appreciation. We learn to be satisfied with what we already have, instead of wanting more. We simplify and downsize our lives by eliminating the need for more. We express appreciation and gratitude for the riches we already possess. Once we learn to "want what we have" instead of "have what we want", our lives become rich and fulfilled.

Learning to Talk, Trust and Feel!

Many of us who were hurt in the past learned three rules: don't talk, don't trust and don't feel. As children we learned to keep secrets, to feel shame and to mistrust. These unwritten rules keep us stuck as adults and prevent others from getting close to us. Sometimes we give our love too much in atonement for our inability to let others get close to us. The only way out of this unhealthy cycle is to break the three rules by talking, trusting and feeling. We can talk to someone with whom we feel safe, a counsellor or a good friend. We can also talk to ourselves by writing our feelings in a journal or talking them out on a tape recorder. We can build trust by learning to trust ourselves first and by feeling our frozen feelings we have locked inside for so long. As we begin to talk, trust and feel we will be blessed with rich and meaningful relationships.

Expressing Joy!

A balanced life requires us to be as open to laughter and humour as well as to pain and sorrow. But some of us take life's challenges so seriously. We think that life has to be all work and no play. Too few of us laugh or smile on the job and we feel guilty having fun. We believe that laughter and joy are exceptions to the rule of getting the job done.

Often we forget to laugh at ourselves, although the potential for fun and happiness is all around us. We overlook the humorous side of life, the funny things children say, a joke someone tells us or the sheer bliss and exhilaration of living. Chuckles, smiles and laughter are as valid as tears, sighs and frowns. A dash of humour adds spice to the humdrum of everyday life. It makes our mental outlook a whole lot brighter and prepares us to begin the day on a positive note.

Take Time to Listen!

We are never alone. Our higher selves and inner power speaks to us every day, whether you are conscious of it or not. That part of the mind in which truth and peace abide is constantly speaking to us. How do we know the difference between our own minds speaking and that of our higher power? Our own mind is that which functions and lives in this world. Much of the time it is disorganized, fearful, uncertain and even chaotic. The part of the mind, which communicates with our higher power is calm, peaceful, certain and fearless. We feel at home there, sit alone on the beach or express our creative abilities. It gives us strength, hope and courage to do the things we need to do in our lives. It never judges or condemns, only encourages and uplifts us. We feel serenity and calm when we speak.

Restoring Our Faith!

Sometimes we find ourselves out of rhythm with the universal process of life because we crowd our mind with fear and anger which distort our world. A spiritual life lets us synchronize ourselves with the universal scheme. We do that by connecting with our spiritual selves.

Too much reason and analysis of our lives can sabotage our spiritual growth. Spirituality cannot be reduced to measureable outcomes under a microscope. When we try to dissect spirituality, it slips through our fingers. Logic and reason and the tools of math and science; faith replaces them as spiritual tools of the spiritual domain. We accept what is, without judgment and logic; and on some days we row and on others we flow.

We become connected to the universal mainstream which sustains us through life's daily challenges. We draw from this spiritual connection to keep ourselves centered.

Fitting In!

How many of us carry the feelings that life is a private club and everyone has a membership card by us? We feel as if we've spent our lives outside looking in. We feel isolated and set apart from others.

Usually these feelings of being cut off from others come from within us. We spend our lives searching for why we are different. We collect evidence for why we don't fit. All of us have a uniqueness that makes us special: yet we are all connected by a universal bond. We are all members of the same emotional and spiritual club. We all are human beings with feelings, feelings that are universal. All of us know the pain of rejection, shame and fears as we know the joy of love, acceptance and happiness.

When our mind sets us apart, our hearts join us together and we are home with ourselves.

Achieving Serenity!

When things don't go our way, it naturally hurts and disappoints us. We may scream and rant and rave. We may even stomp our feet and throw things, like children who don't get their way.

Life runs more smoothly when we accept it as it is, rather than try to make it the way we want. We cannot change the world to fit our whim but we can change how we respond to disappointments by maturely accepting and making the best of them. Trying to change people and situations to meet our terms is time better spent accepting situations as they are.

Being courageous to change those parts of our lives that are changeable and accepting things as they are is the first step to serenity. We can accept the things we cannot change, ask for courage to change the things we can and for the wisdom to know the difference between the two.

· CHAPTER 12 ·

Communicating Clearly

Many of our ways of communicating get tangles and jammed. Perhaps we're afraid to be honest and direct with our feelings. So we either deny that they exist or we communicate them in subtle or indirect ways.

We may drop casual hints, we nonverbal communicators get someone else to speak for us or expect others to read our minds. We can learn to express our emotions honestly and directly. Our frankness with others ensures more open and strife-free relationships. We can untangle the ways in which we relate with people by being kind, direct and honest in what we say and do.

Developing Compassion!

There is a balance between getting over-involved in people's problems and pushing them away. It is important to put the focus on ourselves to grow. It is also important to stop feeling the emotions that belong to others and feel our own. To care for others without taking care of them, but the true test of spiritual development is the ability to get our minds off our egos and develop compassion for others.

Using compassion teaches us to get outside ourselves through another's eyes. When we show compassion we learn to let go of our own rigid point of view and be sensitive to others.

A comment we take can impact someone else's life when we least know it. Doing a kind deed for someone else can change their lives. Empathizing with someone else enriches our own life. In the words of Henry Miller: "until we lose ourselves, there is no hope of finding ourselves."

Shifting Our Outlook

Sometimes life becomes bleak and we feel badly about ourselves. Nothing seems to work the way we mean it to. We try to change the situation, often with little success. The solution is to change our attitude instead of the physical situation. We can create a happy life simply by changing our mental outlook and by looking at our lives in a totally different way. On days when things look gloomy, we can simply change the blurry lens through which we view the world around us. We see more beauty than flaws, more hope than despair. We see good things and optimism even in a loss or a disappointment. We may still get angry and impatient sometimes but our transformation happens on the inside as we look at life from a different slant.

This small grain of knowledge – that we can shift our outlook and change our experience of life – lets us transform our whole existence.

Turning The Worst Into The Best!

Most of us know that negative thinking begets negative situations. The same principle works for us with positive thinking and positive situations. Still, we get caught up in pessimism and catastrophe because that's what we're used to. We can change all that. We don't need to live in a fantasy world of make-believe but we can look for the best in *all* things.

We learn that life is not all misery and drudgery and accept the challenges to transform daily experiences into useful rather than damaging consequences. We turn negative situations around and use them to our advantage. Life experiences become grist for the mill. We use every lesson, no matter how painful or difficult, as a lesson from which to grow.

From now on, we can look at our lives through realistic but optimistic eyes. We can think positive thoughts, feel positive outcomes and the best in life will be ours.

Learning to Bend!

Routines and schedules: we need them to keep our lives orderly. But how many wonderful experiences and people do we exclude by living our lives by the book?

It's time that we look at the limits we put on our lives through our rigidity, refusing to made exceptions to the rules or to bread a mindless routine. Life runs more smoothly when we accept it is it is, rather than trying to make it the way we want.

Spontaneity and flexibility are the ingredients of life satisfaction. Learning to bend with each situation opens our lives to greater happiness. Sometimes this means going against old fears and insecurities and using courage to face life. We conserve more energy, experience greater fulfillment and accomplish more with less frustration and greater ease in the long run.

You have experienced that strong trees are uprooted and blown down when there is a storm in your area, where you live. These are strong trees and some are big and mighty, they are proud and strong and are joy to your neighbourhood, these beautiful trees went down with the storm because they are stubborn and don't want to bend.

When you see a storm in the tropics, with many palm and coconut trees, not many of these trees are blown down. Why? Because they bend, they go with the flow, so to speak.

Some of us, maybe you to, are like the strong proud trees, we stand our ground, and we don't want to give in. We are always right, the stubborn me, I don't care, I don't negotiate, and there you are, you will lose and be blown down like that strong stubborn tree.

Learn to bend a little like the palm tree, bend a little in your personal life, your work life, your career, your social life, your political life, and special in your thinking to avoid the hardening of your attitude.

Embracing Our Good!

All of us have heard the expression "it's better to give than to receive", still we get caught up in our own needs and spend so much time taking, that we cannot participate in the giving and receiving process.

We are more accustomed to holding on to what we want than we are of letting go. Our way of life teaches us to possess rather than to give. So we are more likely to cling to take than to give up and let go.

As good comes to us, we must let it go in order to keep it. The good feeling we get from doing little things for others outweighs the good deed. Self-gratification comes from giving freely and fully out of love and the desire to share.

Sharing and doing good deeds are not done with expectations. They are given freely from the heart, because it feels natural and right.

CHAPTER 13

Success

Success is a belief. We can have failure consciousness or success consciousness. It will take the same amount of energy.

You have to learn how the conscious works. The conscious works by relaxing your mind and body, when you calm yourself you find that the chaos is in your mind, that will slow but surely lessen, and you get it, control over your life. It has to start with your mind: when you control your head (mind) things will change, it is all a matter of attitude.

Your mind is a "thought factory". It is a busy factory producing all kinds of thoughts every day, every hour and every minute. In the thought factory there are two supervisors, one of them is called Mr. Success the other is called Mr. Failure. Mr. Success is in charge of manufacturing positive thoughts, he produces reasons why you can, why you're qualified, why you can and will. The other supervisor, Mr. Failure, produces negative, deprecating thoughts, he is the expert in developing reasons why you can't succeed, and that you are weak and not good enough, his specialty is "why you will fail".

Both Mr. Success and Mr. Failure are very obedient, they snap at attention right away all you need to do, is signal either supervisor, or give the slightest mental beckoning call. When the signal is positive, Mr. Success will step forward and go to work, and a negative signal brings Mr. Failure forward and he will go to work.

To see how these supervisors work for you, try this example: tell yourself, "Today is a lousy day." This signals Mr. Failure into action and he manufactures some facts to prove you are right. He suggests to you that it's too hot or too cold, business will be bad today, sales will drop, other people will be on edge, some may get sick, your spouse will be in a bad mood. Mr. Failure is very efficient. In just a few moments he got you sold, and it is a bad day. Before you know it, it is a heck of a bad day. Then tell yourself: "Today is a fine day", and Mr. Success is signalled to more forward to act accordingly. He tells you, "this is a wonderful day, the weather is refreshing, it is good to be alive" then it is a good day.

In life fashion Mr. Failure can show how you can't sell to Smith. Mr. Success will show you that you can and will sell to Smith. Mr. Failure will convince you that you will fail, while Mr. Success will demonstrate why you can and will succeed.

Mr. Failure will prepare a brilliant case against Tom, while Mr. Success will show you more reasons why you like Tom.

Now the more work you give either of these two supervisors, the stronger he becomes. If Mr. Failure is given more work to do he will take more space in your mind. Eventually, he will take over the entire thought division and virtually all thoughts will be of a negative nature. The only wise thing to do is **fire Mr. Failure**! You don't need him around telling you what you can't do, that you're not up to it, that you'll fail, and so on. Mr. Failure won't help you get where you want to go, so, **boot him out**!

Use Mr. Success all the time, when thoughts enter your mind, ask Mr. Success to go to work for you, he'll show you how you can succeed.

Between now and tomorrow a few hundred new Canadians will arrive in our great country. Canada's population is growing at record rates, and over the next ten years this will mean millions more people. New industries, new scientific breakthroughs, expanding markets – all spell opportunities. This is good news, this is a most wonderful time to be alive, all signs point to a record demand for top-level people in every field, people who have superior abilities to influence others, to direct their work, and to serve in leadership capacity. And the people who fill these leadership positions are all adults or near adults **right now**, and one of them is <u>you</u>!

The guarantee of a boom is not, of course, a guarantee of personal success over the long haul. Canada always has been a successful country. But just a fast glance shows that millions and millions of people – in fact, a majority of them – struggle and don't really succeed. The majority of folks still plug along, they struggle but don't succeed or live their dream, despite the record opportunities of the last two or three decades, and in the boom period ahead, most people will continue to worry, to be afraid, and will crawl through life feeling unimportant, unappreciated, and not able to do what they want to do. As a result, their performances will earn them petty rewards – petty happiness.

Those who convert opportunities into rewards (and let me say) I sincerely believe you are one of those people, or else you would not have bought my book, you are one of those people who learn to think for themselves and to succeed.

Motivation: The Driving Force

The person determined to achieve maximum success learns the principle that progress is made one step at a time. A home is built one brick at a time. Football games are won, or lost, one play at a time. A store grows with one customer at a time. A lot of little accomplishments become a big accomplishment. A nail driven into a plank, takes more than one hammer blow.

I read a story sometime ago in the Readers' Digest, and here is part of it:

During WWII, I (not me) and several other soldiers had to parachute from a crippled army transport plane into the mountainous jungles of the Burma-India border. It could be several weeks before an armed relief expedition could reach us, so we started to walk "out" to civilized India. We were faced with a 140 mile trek, over mountains, in the August heat and monsoon rains. On the first day I had already blisters the size of fifty-cent pieces on both feet.

Could I hobble 140 miles? Could the others, some in worse shape than I, complete such a distance? We were convinced we could not. But we could hobble to that ridge, we could make it to the next friendly Indian village for the night, and that, of course, was **all** we had to do.

The soldiers also took one day and one step at a time, and like in this story you made decisions, one day at a time when you are moving forward in your life. Tough things and times don't last, but .... tough people do!!

You have to constantly see the goal you want to reach, you also have to earn that goal. Nothing will happen if you sit on the couch all the time and expect your ultimate goal to be delivered to you on a silver platter, if you do, **you are dreaming in Technicolor.**

Keep the subconscious mind working for you, instruct it. Relax your thought and things will happen, I do not promise this, I guarantee it!

When you want a better job or a raise from your employer, don't keep griping and complaining with your co-worker, change your tune. To get a promotion or a raise, all you have to do is increase your knowledge and surpass your own ability, you don't have to beat the other person just do better than before, and you will succeed.

A young man, at a seminar in Sudbury mentioned his need for a piece of garden, so he and his wife could work the soil and grow their own veggies, etc... At lunch time he was at a table for six persons, and one man asked if it was him who mentioned this garden plot, yes he said: "That was I". This gentleman was a farmer, and he had a ¼ acre of land that had been cut off his land when the county widened the road, and right then and there he gladly sold this piece of land to this young man and his wife for the price of $1.00.

You see strange things happen to good people with a simple need, and once you give your subconscious instruction and stick to it, it will give you whatever you need. You know we all want lots and lots of money but we are not willing to sacrifice one little iota.

Making a Good Brain Great!

I have been teaching seminars and weekly mediation classes in many places in Canada and the USA. I wrote booklets about meditation and relaxation, and a weight loss program. For years my friends told me to write a book about myself and my experiences (I have a colourful life) but I decided to write this one first, because I believe that this book will help people. You don't know how easy it is to upgrade your life, your career, and your happiness.

Today 50% of marriages and common-law relationships break up because of decisions we made years prior, because we didn't think this out. Of the other 50% that stay together only 10% are happy campers, so all the others stay together for children, financial commitment, or they dislike each other so much, they don't want to give their partner freedom and a chance of a new life.

Let's wake up and smell the roses let's change our "stinking thinking, to avoid the hardening of the attitude". I believe that too many people have cement shoes and stay in a mould that is not good for them and the people they are suppose to be close to.

Make something of your life, make changes. We don't laugh enough, but cry and complain too much. We have more degrees, but less common sense. We have learned to make a living but not how to live life. We have added years to life, but we have not added life to the years. We have more medicine, but less wellness.

Like an ostrich with it's' head in the sand, we are hiding from our own problems, crossing our fingers, and hoping things will get better. We need to take our heads out of the sand, take action to solve our own problems and go back to the principles of living a good, honest life. The very existence of the family is in danger, through divorce, abuse, drugs, alcohol, adultery and materialism, the list goes on and on.

"Life has challenges and opportunities". I will change your life and the way you think about problems for the rest of your life. Everybody has problems large and small, most people make mountains out of mole hills! So we have to work hard to solve them.

I know of a place, right where you live, and the people who go there have no problems at all, their problems are over, that place is your local cemetery. You can look around you, talk to your friends and families and you find most of the problems large and small are self-imposed. In other words it is your own damn fault! S.I.W. "Self Imposed Wounds"

You can point your index finger at other people and blame them for your problems; it is my parent's fault, my teacher's fault, my spouse's fault, my boss' fault. Now I want you to look at your own hand, when you point that finger, take a good hard look, because three fingers are looking right back at you! You create most of your problems yourself, in other words, it is your own damn fault because you failed to plan, so…you plan to fail.

The Source

Separated from the source, the source of life, you lose the power of yourself, to negotiate with yourself, to get yourself back to your plan of life. You are connected to your thoughts, the way to reason with your conscious and subconscious mind.

You are able to control your life by creating a plan to succeed, you have to learn to talk to yourself, release the negative forces that are around you, that hold you down and start controlling your thought force to get ahead and stars reaching for your ultimate goal.

You have to recognize that your thoughts are yours to direct and control, you think negative and the result will be negative, change your thoughts to positive, good things will automatically occur, that is the Law of Life!

It may take a bit of time to remove all your negative thoughts from your head and your life, but the rewards are worth it. You have to understand that bad things happen to bad people, bad things happen to good people also. You have to accept this and move on with Life, "bad things don't last, but people do. You have to accept this and go on as best you can, maybe change direction and of course you are allowed U turns.

You can't keep beating a dead horse, as they say. The young people say "suck it up", sure, sure you will say that is easier said than done, but you can't keep on moping and complaining all the time, you will get depressed and out of sorts, your food doesn't taste the same, you can't sleep properly, because you thought force is out of sink, every action creates a re-action.

The Process of Getting Ahead Sooner

We have to accept the fact that all of life has it's ups and downs, because we get results, bad or good, from decisions we made a few years back, we then made the right or wrong decision, and now the chickens are coming home to roost, so they say. Next time around, make sure you really think about it, when you have to make a decision, it could affect your life in the long run.

Don't think I did not have ups and downs in my own life, I have a broken marriage, I had a very busy business some years ago, and I lost my shirt, so to speak, and it took me four years of hard physical work to pay all my bills, because I could not see myself going bankrupt. After that period in my life, I started talking to people and asking myself "why do bad things happen to good people?"

I started to read good positive books, went to lectures, weekend seminars, learned mediation and slow but sure my life changed, because my thought force changed, it changed so much, that I myself started to teach what I learned over a period of five years , and for the past forty years I have been doing, lectures and seminars to people of all walks of life and have been invited to many T.V. and radio shows.

This all happened to me because I was crying out for help and help I found, so much so that it changed my life totally, I made that U Turn, you to are allowed to make this U turn. Do it today, "Today it the first day of the rest of your new life!"

Success Motivation

Several years ago, I was brought face to face with the very disturbing realization that I was trying to supervise and direct the efforts of a large number of people who were trying to achieve success, without knowing myself what the secret of success really was. That, naturally, brought me face to face with the further realization that regardless of what other knowledge I might have brought to my job, I as definitely lacking in the most important knowledge of all.

Of course, like most of us, I had been brought up on the popular belief that the secret of success is hard work, but, I had seen so many men work hard without succeeding and so many men succeed without working hard, that I had become convinced that hard word was not the real secret even though in most cases it might be one of the requirements.

So, I set out on a voyage of discovery which carried me through biographies and autobiographies and all sorts of dissertations on success and the lives of successful men until I finally reached a point at which I realized that the secret I was trying to discover lay not only in what men did, but, also in what made them do it.

I realized further that the secret for which I was searching must not apply to every definition of success, but, since it must apply to everyone to whom it was offered, it must also apply to everyone who had ever been successful. In short, I was looking for the common denominator or success.

Because that is exactly what I was looking for, that is exactly what I found.

The Process of Getting Ahead Sooner

This common denominator of success is so big, so powerful and so vitally important to your future and mine that I'm just going to "lay it on the line" in words of one syllable, so simple that everyone can understand them.

The common denominator of success ... the secret of success of every man or woman who has ever been successful ... lies in the fact that he formed the habit of doing things that failures don't like to do.

If the secret of success lies in forming the habit of doing things that failures don't like to do, let's start the boiling down process by determining what are the things that failures don't like to do! The things that failures don't like to do are the very things that you and I and other human beings, including successful men, naturally don't like to do. In other words, we've got to realize right from the start that success is something which is achieved by the minority of men and it, therefore, uncommon and not to be achieved by following our natural likes and dislikes, nor by being guided by our natural preferences and prejudices.

The things that failures don't like to do, in general, are too many and too obvious for us to discuss them here, and so, since our success is to be achieved in life, let us move on to a discussion of the things that we as individuals don't like to do. Here too, the things we don't like to do are too many to permit a specific discussion, but, i think they can all be disposed of by saying that they all emanate from one basic dislike peculiar to life. We don't like to take the time to look inside the truly examine ourselves – to be honest with ourselves and critical of our weaknesses to establish what we need to do to strengthen our characters – to examine what we really want out of life and how important it is to establish what price we are prepared to pay to achieve it.

It will still explain why people have gone through life with every apparent qualification of success and still ended up as disappointing failures, while others have achieved outstanding success in spite of many obvious and discouraging handicaps .

Since it might also explain your future, it would seem to be a mighty good idea for you to use it in determining just what sort of a future you are going to have. In other words, let's take this big, all embracing secret and boil it down to fit the individual you.

Perhaps you have been discouraged by a feeling that you were born subject to certain dislikes peculiar to you, with which the successful people are not afflicted. Perhaps you have wondered why it is that the most successful people seem to like to do the things that you don't like to do.

They don't, and I think this is the most encouraging statement I have ever offered to anyone.

If they don't like to do these things, then why do they do them? Because by doing the things they don't like to do, they can accomplish the things they want to accomplish. Successful people are influenced by the desire for pleasing results. Failures are influenced by the desire for pleasing methods and are inclined to be satisfied with such results as can be obtained by doing things they like to do.

Why are successful people able to do the things they don't like to do while failures are not? Because successful people have a purpose strong enough to make them form the habit of doing things they don't like to do in order to accomplish the purpose they want to accomplish.

Sometimes even the best of us get into a slump. When a person goes into a slump, it simply means that they have reached a point at which, for the time being, the things they don't like to do have become more important than their reasons for doing them. Anyway, I pause to suggest to you that should you go into a slump, the less you talk about why you are in a slump and the more your talk is about your purpose, the sooner you will pull yourself out of the slump.

Many men with whom I have discussed this common denominator of success have said at this point: "But, I have a family to support and I have to earn a living for my family and myself. Isn't that enough of a purpose?" No, it is not. It isn't a sufficiently strong purpose to make you form the habit of doing the things you don't like to do for the very simple reason that it is easier to adjust ourselves to the hardships of a poor living than it is to adjust ourselves to the hardships of making a better one. If you doubt me, just think of all the things you are willing to go without in order to avoid doing the things you don't like to do. All of which seems to prove that the strength which holds you to your purpose if not your own strength, but the strength of the purpose itself.

Now, let's see why habit belongs so importantly in this common denominator of success.

Every single qualification for success is acquired through habit. People form habits and habits form futures. If you do not deliberately form good habits, then unconsciously you will form bad ones. You are the kind of a person you are because you have formed the habit of being that kind of person, and the only way you can change is through habit.

The success habits can be divided into four main areas:

1. Personal
2. Family
3. Social
4. Vocational

Before you decide to adopt these success habits, let me warn you of the importance of habit to your decision. I have attended many meetings during the past ten years and have often wondered why, in spite of the fact that there is so much good in them, so many people seem to get so little good out of them. Perhaps you have attended meetings in the past and have left these meetings determined to do the things that would make you successful or more successful, only to find your decision or determination waning at just the time when it should be put into effect or practice.

Here's the answer. Any resolution or decision you make is simply a promise to yourself which isn't worth a tinker's damn until you have formed the habit of making it and keeping it. You won't form the habit of making it and keeping it unless right at the start, you link it with a definite purpose that can be accomplished by keeping it. In other words, any resolution or decision you make today has to be make again tomorrow, and the next day, and the next, and the next, and so on. It not only has to be make each day, but, it has to be kept each day. For, if you miss one day in the making or keeping it, you're got to go back and begin all over again. If you continue the process of making it each morning, and keeping it each day, you will finally wake up some morning, a different person in a different world, and you will wonder that has happened to you and the world you used to live in.

Here's what happened. Your resolution or decision has become a habit and you don't have to make it on this particular morning. The reason for your seeming like a different person living in a different world lies in the fact that for the first time in your life, you have become master of yourself, and master of your likes and dislikes, by surrendering to your purpose in life. That is why behind every success there must be a purpose and that is what makes purpose so important to your future. For in the last analysis, your future is not going to depend on economic conditions or outside influences or circumstances over which you have no control.

Your future is going to depend on your purpose in life. So, let's talk about purpose.

First of all, your purpose must be practical and not visionary. Some time ago, I talked with a man who thought he had a purpose which was more important to him than income. He was interested in the sufferings of his fellow-man, and he wanted to be placed in a position to alleviate that suffering. When we analyzed his real feelings, we discovered, and he admitted it, that what he really wanted was a real nice job dispensing charity with other people's money and being well paid for it, along with the appreciation and feeling of importance what would naturally to with such a job.

In making your purpose practical, be careful not to make it logical. Make it a purpose of the sentimental or emotional type. Remember needs are logical while wants and desires are sentimental and emotional. Your needs will push you just so far, but, when your needs are satisfied, they will stop pushing you. If, however, your purpose is in terms of wants or desires, then, your wants and desires will keep pushing you long after your needs are satisfied and until your wants and desires are fulfilled.

Recently, I was talking with a young man who long ago discovered the common denominator of success without identifying his discovery. He had a definite purpose in life and it was definitely a sentimental or emotional purpose. He wanted his boy to go through college without having to work his way through as he had done. He wanted to avoid for his little girl the hardships which his own sister had had to face in her childhood. He wanted his wife and the mother of his children to enjoy the luxuries and comforts, and even necessities, which had been denied his own mother. He was willing to form the habit of doing things he didn't like to do in order to accomplish this purpose.

Not to discourage him, but rather to have him encourage me, I said to him: "Aren't you going just a little too far with this thing? There is no logical reason why your son shouldn't be willing and able to work his way through college just as his father did. Of course, he'll miss many of the things that you missed in your college life and he'll probably have heartaches and disappointments, but, if he's any good, he'll come through in the end just as you did. There's no logical reason why you should slave in order that you daughter may have things which your own sister wasn't able to have, or in order that your wife can enjoy comforts and luxuries that she wasn't used to before she married you."

He looked at me with rather a pitying look and said: "But, there's no inspiration in logic. There's no courage in logic. There's not even happiness in logic. There's only satisfaction. The only place logic has in my life is in the realization that the more I am willing to do for my wife and children, the more I shall be able to do for myself."

I imagine after hearing that story, you won't have to be told how to find your purpose or how to identify it or how to surrender to it. If it's a big purpose, you will be big in its accomplishment. If it's an unselfish purpose, you will be unselfish in accomplishing it. If it's an honest purpose, you will be honest and honourable in the accomplishment of it.

As long as you live, don't ever forget that while you may succeed beyond your fondest hopes and your greatest expectations, you will never succeed beyond the purpose to which you are willing to surrender. Furthermore, your surrender will not be complete until you have formed the habit of doing the things that failures don't like to do.

It's just as true as it sounds and it's just as simple as it seems. You can hold it up to the light, you can put it to the acid test, and you can kick it around until it's worn out, but, when you are all through with it, it will still be the common denominator or success, whether we like it or not.

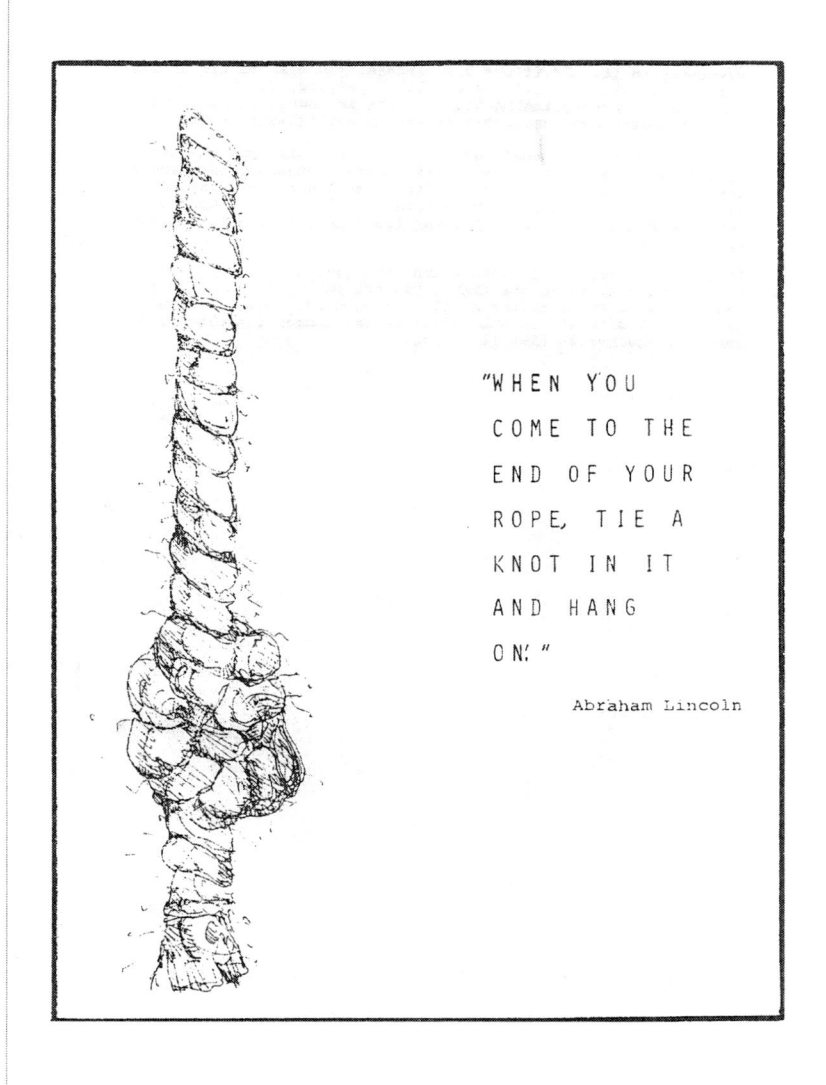

"WHEN YOU COME TO THE END OF YOUR ROPE, TIE A KNOT IN IT AND HANG ON."

Abraham Lincoln

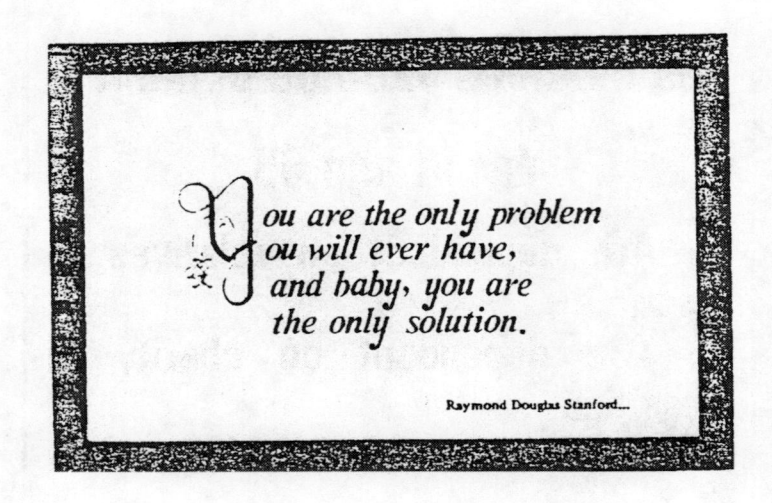

> You are the only problem
> you will ever have,
> and baby, you are
> the only solution.
>
> Raymond Douglas Stanford...

85 Out of every 100 men

Reaching age 65 do not possess as much as $250.00 cash

Yet at age 65
45% Are dependent on relatives for assistance
30% Are dependent on charity for necessities
23% Still have to work for a living
2% And only 2% are self-sustaining

Only 3 out of 10 in the top income brackets ($50,000.00 and up) can quit work at the age of 65

THE INCOMES OF DOCTORS, LAWYERS AND MOST PROFESSIONS ON AN AVERAGE START TOPPING OFF AT AGE 47 AND PLUNGE RAPIDLY AFTER 54.

Fewer men are worth $100 at age 68 than at 18 after 50 years of hard work.

· CHAPTER 14 ·

"The Science"

Years ago I saw a television interview with Mr. Liberachy. The interviewee asked "when did you first know that your great success was real"? the answer changed my life Liberachy said: "I have a book called The Magic of Believing", he went on to explain that he had 3 copies: one in his suitcase for when he travels, one on his night table, and one on his coffee table. He opens the book at least once a day and reads that page or Chapter, and it changed his life!

As a matter of fact, I have 2 copies and read some of it each and every day, my friends; the secret is repeat reading that's when things start to change for you. Remember when you were at school, you learned by repeating 2+2 makes 4, 4+4 makes 8, C A T spells cat, D O G spells dog. They kept telling you until it got you or you got it!

You go to the store, and get the product that looks familiar to you because it was advertised by the old formula of repeating.

This is what this science is all about "Repeating". Good stuff. I want you to take six pieces of paper, the size of a business card, any color will do. I want you to stick them to places you see all the time. For instance, where you make your tea or coffee, one in the bathroom, one on your bed, one on the mirror where you shave or do your make-up or comb your hair, one on your desk or worktable, one on the dashboard of your car, one on your door at your house or apartment, and one in your wallet.

Now, what I want you to do is spend some time by yourself, an hour or two if you can. Maybe go for a walk in the park. If you like driving, go for a drive, just be by yourself to get your mind to go into neutral, like a car that stops at a red light. The car is in neutral, but the engine still runs smoothly. I'd like you to put a six month's desire and need in your thought pattern. Something you'd like to receive, a goal you'd like to reach, something you need. Now break it down to one month steps. Be Clear. Don't be wishy washy. Make it clear, one step at a time. Relax yourself, breath a bit slower, see your aim clearly. Don't look at what we want, look at what you <u>need</u>. When you are done, put your thoughts on the cards. Mentally keep it to yourself. This is <u>your</u> project. Don't share it with anyone.

When your cards are all in place, what you need to do is, when you see one of your cards, you say mentally, "I know it will come to me". Do this at least 40 or more times a day.

What you are doing is your repeating your desire, is telling your subconscious to go to work for you and fulfill your need. You have to understand that the repeating works just the same as when you were a child learning the 2+2=4 etc.

The subconscious has to be trained. Once it is locked in your subconscious, **ALL** things come to you.

In my seminars, I ask the participants the questions of what they need, and all kinds of desires are expressed. One lady needed a car, and I told her how to go about it. The same as I have told you. Three days later, the lady had a car out of the blue! This case is not an exception. Most things do take a bit longer, it all depends how you get your mind to work for you, and how strong your determination is. Don't start thinking about how it will come to you, just go for it.

I don't know if you have children, or remember your childhood. Small children maybe 2 or 3 years old, want a cookie.

The Process of Getting Ahead Sooner

The mom says "not now baby, maybe later when you The child starts to cry and stomp their feet. They cookie, and usually the parent gives in to stop the crying.

Now, the child does not know if the cookie is bought, b , given or stolen. All the child wants is that cookie. This is how you have to become. Expect things to happen for you, straight forward, deserving, and amazing things will come to you, be determined and strong about it.

Don't start analyzing how it will or can come to you, or how your need will be fulfilled. Be like a child with a cookie. Tell your subconscious mind over and over, with the help of your cards, that whatever you need will come to you.

You have to understand that your subconscious mind needs to be trained, and that is done by your repetitions over and over. I have seen this science work for many, many people. They stick to their need and trained their subconscious mind to make it work for them. Of course, everybody has to start with some sense of "How do I make it work for me"? Let me give you a simple start that will give you confidence in yourself.

I don't drive a car, my choice. A friend of mine, Donna, and I were going to an evening performance at our downtown theatre called "Showplace", Donna was going to pick me up and we were both attending the stand-up comedy show. Donna called me to say she was delayed and would pick me up at 7:30 pm. This made it very tight, time wise, as the show started at 8:00 pm. And, of course, parking would be at a premium, but I was not worried about the parking at all because when I am in a car with someone, there is always a legal parking spot for me. So when Donna and I came near the theatre, a car pulled out and we pulled in that "legal" parking space! And we were only about fifty steps from the front door!

How is this done? It is the same science I told you about. All you have to do is feel deserving. I would like to start you with this simple parking space science. It could give you the confidence and you can see for yourself that this system works. Start with something simple like a parking spot.

133

Let me say that you have to go to a very busy place with lots of cars on the road and not a lot of parking spots, Okay! Now, when you put your car key in the ignition, say to yourself, "I will have a parking spot within one block from my destination". Say this three or four times, and I guarantee you will have that spot!

I like to go out for dinner with my friends on a Saturday or Sunday evening. You know as well as I do that these are busy times for restaurants. So, of course, where do we park? When I was in your car you would probably find a place very near the front door. Sounds funny, right? But I have trained my subconscious mind for years. You have to learn it is like anything else in life. When something comes along, you have to study it, learn it and practice. Remember – Your mind is like a parachute, it only works when it is <u>open</u>!

Many people are set in a pattern in life. They always do the same things all the time. They might shower at the same time each day or they eat the same breakfast, they comb their hair the same way every day. They play golf, tennis, go to the gym, etc., etc. the same things at the same time. You can't get them to change. I am asking you to change a little. Get off of this track you are on. Yes, you move around but the same circle makes you sad and restless. Instead, drive a different route when you go to work, smile a little more often, go to a different place for dinner, meet new people, join a card club or bowling league, go dancing. Remember when you were a little younger, how you loved to dance and have fun? Start to do the things you loved to do a few years ago. You got a bit in a rut and it is good sometimes to change the pace a little.

As you know, I live in Peterborough, Ontario, which is a great city. We have an area near where I live called Jackson Park. I go there a few times a week for a little stroll. I like nature; it is good to get some fresh air. There is a creek in this park called Jackson Creek. The water is low in the summer and I see parents and their children playing around they're trying to catch some small fish. It is a great place for family fun time, people walking, bicycling, running, etc. It is a gorgeous playground, right in the heart of our city. Most people here know about it but never get there because they are too busy. I know, I know, we have to make a living and all that stuff. But you have to take time out too just to see how the other half lives.

What I am trying to tell you is this: get off your own carousel. Stop and smell the roses. Make a few small efforts, try something new. Give yourself a break once in a while. You will find that your work, business, household, etc., will become more enjoyable. You hear some people say that they are taking time off to go somewhere to clear their mind. This is what I mean when I say "take a break sometimes", to clear your head. We have lots of problems but they are usually our own doing. Take stock sometimes. Let your thoughts tell you where you troubles lie, then take them seriously.

A man I know had lots of problems but never tried to solve them. He had a heart attack and died at the age of forty-two. You have to understand that the troubles in your head have a <u>great</u> effect on your physical health.

Pressure, depression, hyper tension, etc, mostly created in your mind, this is why part of my book is titled, "A Check Up From the Neck Up". When you can resolve all this chaos in your mind, you can avoid high blood pressure, improve your sleep, cut anxiety, ease hyper-tension, reduce pain, correct eating disorders, etc. all these problems start in your mind, like a thought factory. Change your thoughts and you will change your life. I want you to get away from the negative cycle you may be in. Give thanks for the things you have accomplished. You're not stupid, there must be some good stuff planted in your head, things you have learned through living and repetition.

I believe that adult life starts when we are twenty years old. Anything before that is kids stuff though the youngsters don't think so; they like to tell their parents what life is all about. Children will grow up to realize the reality of life. From the age of twenty until thirty five are the learning years. This is when we learn our trades and become craftsmen and craftswomen. This is the time we go to college and university. Then we are ready to tackle the world and make a living. You are now in the working world. Now you have to practice what you learned. It all feels very strange because now you have to produce. All this learning is over, school is out! Now you have to prove what you are made of. What kind of character are you? Are you able to give orders or take orders? You have to be on time on the job. You don't sleep in anymore. You can't cancel a class. What are you made of? Do you have the stuff to succeed? When you are any good, and I know deep inside of me that you are, you will succeed. And some off you lead this beautiful country of ours in the future.

The age of thirty five to fifty are your power years. This is where the super smart ones will go up in their chosen careers. They are the ones who carry great responsibilities on their shoulders. These people have the right stuff to lead. This is when the artist has breakthroughs in their chosen field. This is where the construction worker looks at his/her building and feels proud of their accomplishment. You may not know it but you are one of the building blocks of the country. You make it work through good and bad times. Be proud of what you do and do it well!

Let me tell you something; "do you know that ten percent of people make things happen, another ten percent of people understand what is happening and eighty percent of people don't know or understand what the hell is happening!"

Brian & Linda

I met a couple, Brian and Linda, in Syracuse, NY, on one of my seminars. They invited me to Sunday dinner, which I gratefully accepted. The food and company were great. When we came to dessert, Brian told me he wanted to show me something and this is his story!

When Brian and Linda were engaged, they often talked about having their own home, like many young couples do. Brian is a very smart man and started to draw their dream home. The layout included the location of the bedrooms, the kitchen, and the stairs to the basement, the living room and the dining room, etc., etc.

For twelve years, they tried to save some money but there were obstacles along the way. First, Brian was out of work for three months. Linda needed doctor's care and spent a week in the hospital. Two years later, their second baby was born. So, the savings were used for things at hand. By the time I met them, they had three children. Brian had a good steady job and Linda stayed at home as she liked to raise her family. They managed very well but they could not afford to buy a house of their own. They often talked about their dream home and kept it in their thoughts.

Brian and Linda are "family" people. Everything they did revolved around their family, including extended family and parents, in other words, a close-knit family. On summer weekends they loaded up their station wagon with family and goodies and went for picnics in the country. One of those trips in the country; they saw a house with a "for sale by owner" sign. They drove by it but Linda persisted, she wanted to look at the home so Brian turned the car around and went back to the house.

The door opened after they rang the bell and they asked if it was convenient to see the place. It was okay and in they went. They went from the first room to another, to the kitchen. Brian looked at Linda and Linda stared at Brian as this house was exactly the same as their dream home that they had discussed and drawn on paper twelve years ago. There was one difference. The house had parking for three cars and Brian's drawing had space for only one. Talk about me being so excited, whoohoo, when Brian showed me the drawing of the dream house, and the edges were a bid discoloured and curled up, and there it was, the proof of the thought forces. It is proof of the old saying, "if you fail to plan, you plan to fail".

The people who sold the house to them were retiring to Florida, to get away from the cold winters. They gave Brian and Linda a great deal; no down payment and their monthly payment would be a payment to the house.

The reason I told you the Brian Linda story is to show you that things you dream about consistently will come to you! Big things may take a bit longer but when the time is right and you are ready to receive it, it will fall into your lap! Again I tell you, the "science" with the five or six cards works all the time. It is people who fail the science!

· CHAPTER 15 ·

Club La Vie

When I was about twelve or thirteen my parents suggested that I take ballroom dancing lessons to build social structure that is good for later in life, so you don't become a wall flower. I took to ballroom dancing like a duck takes to water, I love to sway to the music and feel relaxed and music takes you to a different world.

On May 10th 1940 the German Hitler machine invaded Holland (my birth country) and they occupied us for five years, it also was the end of my dancing, at that time!

When I was in my late thirties I found myself single again, and on weekends I sometimes went to dances for relaxation and the joy of music. I was living in Toronto at the time, and did not like the music the people and the set up, and most of them (the dances) were meat markets.

So, crazy me, I started my own dances, I rented the ballroom from the Howard Johnson Hotel at the 401 and Markham Rd, and hired a good D.J. on a weekly basis. I started advertising, put flyers on cars and mailboxes, I hired 5 men and 5 women to be a host and hostesses, and off it went. It was very slow for the first 5 months and I invested about $35,000.00 to get it going.

But going it did and I never looked back and I was getting good crowds of 250 – 300 people.

On February the 14th 1996 the Toronto Star daily newspaper (Business Section) wrote a story about "Club La Vie" and here it is. By John Picton Special to the Toronto Star.

IN THE SWING: It was a long time between dances, but social-club operator Jack Deurloo is back in the twirl, with disc jockey Marlene Hamilton.

The Toronto Star Wednesday, February 14, 1996

Fancy footwork now his business
Get-togethers going strong at Deurloo's dances

By John Picton
Special to the Star

Jack Deurloo had hardly danced since before those dark days in World War II when he was a courier in the Dutch underground movement.

Then, as a teenager, he carried secret messages from cell to cell, his forged paper declaring his date of birth as 1928, not 1926, so he would appear too young to be sent to Germany as slave labour.

At home, his three older brothers were hiding out in the attic so they wouldn't be shipped to fatal work details, either.

On the streets, his painter father, who was an air-raid warden, forged copies of the arm bank he'd been issued and distributed them to those eligible for shipment, giving the potential victims time to hide.

Anyone wearing the bands could walk the streets unchallenged during daylight hours.

Deurloo had been taking dance lessons until the German occupation, but that stopped along with little electricity even for lighting.

So, it was 1984 before he took up dancing seriously again.

That was the year he started the Club la Vie (Club of Life), a Scarborough-based club where people can get together for social evenings.

It was the year he retired from his painting and contracting business to do just that.

"I decided to start a club for people where they could safely got to know compatible people without embarrassment", says Deurloo, 69.

"People coming out of a relationship with family responsibilities often find it very difficult to meet other people on a social basis without a substantial risk".

Club la Vie, which operates from rented halls, employs one person full-time and five part-time and took in $200,000.00 in sales last year.

The club operates on Friday and Saturday nights.

"We get between 250 and 300 people on Friday nights, and we average 120 – 150 on Saturdays", Deurloo says. "On special nights, we are up to 375.

And over all these years, I've only had to cut off about 12 people at the bar".

Entry is $10.00, which includes a buffet dinner.

On a recent night, guest Michael Ziny commented, "they are very nice and friendly people and they're good dances. You can't beat that, and a meal, for $10".

Said Shirley from Whitby, "I love the club because it's so friendly with great music and almost everyone is dressed to impress. I just hate to go to places where they're wearing jeans".

Added Donna from Oshawa, "there are four of us who usually go every week and we go for a good time because it's just like a party".

The music is played by disc hockey Marlene Hamilton is, under the name Doctor Music, has been a regular at the club for almost seven years.

Why did Deurloo start the club?

"I sold my ... business in 1981 and I was doing nothing," he says.

"I liked dancing and went to dances, and I felt I could create a better atmosphere for people. In some cases, dancers didn't even know who was in charge, and I liked the thought of the public relations".

"In many cases, there was no one to greet people and shake their hands."

• CHAPTER 16 •

Physically Hungry – Eat

Question, please! Did you eat anything last month? What about last week? Yesterday? Today? Chances are you are quite puzzled at these questions. Of course you ate last month, last week, yesterday and today. Do you plan to eat tomorrow? If you do, does that mean what you ate today was not good? Absolutely not, it simply means what you ate today is for today. The average person in Canada not only eats every day, but generally speaking, he eats his meals on schedule. I've observed if a person gets busy and misses a meal, he generally tells anyone who will listen, "You know what? I was so busy yesterday that I didn't have time to eat lunch". Then he repeats it to make certain his listener got the message. To him, it's a big deal to miss a meal and he wants others to be aware of his "sacrifice". Suppose the same individual was asked about his mental appetites? When is the last time you deliberately, on a pre-determined schedule, fed your own mind? What do you think his answer would be? For that matter – what is YOUR answer? Your answer is important because you have mental appetites just as you have physical appetites.

Mentally Hungry – What do you do?

People are funny. I've never met an individual who was hungry and heard him say: "I'm about to starve. I wonder what I should do? Do you have any suggestions? Can you give me an idea how to solve this problem?" I probably never will be confronted with that particular situation. The hungry person knows if he's hungry, he can solve that problem by eating.

From the neck down, very few people are worth more than $100.00 a week. From the neck up, there is no limit to what an individual is worth. So what do we do? We feed our stomachs, the $100.00 part below our necks, every day. How often do we feed our minds, the part that has no limit to its value, earning and happiness potential? Most of us feed it accidentally and occasionally, if it's convenient or we don't have anything else to do. The excuse we often give is lack of time. This is ridiculous. If you have time to feed the $100.00 part of you every day, doesn't it make sense you should TAKE time to feed the part which has no ceiling to its potential? On many occasions, I have encountered people who are despondent, negative, defeated, down on themselves, broke, unhappy and you name it. If it's on the negative side, it will fit them. The funny thing about these people is that they're the ones who resist to the bitter end, any feeding of their minds or their attitudes. They badly need inspiration and information but, they consistently refuse to attend seminars or get involved in reading books or listening to motivational recordings. It's really funny to listen to some of these people talk – perhaps I should use the work "tragic"?

When we refer to extremely successful people and mention how optimistic and positive they are, the failure will say: "No wonder they're positive and have good attitudes, they are earning $100,000.00 a year, I would be positive too." The failure thinks successful people are positive because they earn $100,000.00 a year. This is in reverse. Successful people earn $100,000.00 a year because they have the RIGHT MENTAL ATTITUDE. Wouldn't it be marvellous if it had been arranged so that an empty stomach wouldn't let its owner rest until its owner put something in it?

It's true in every field of endeavour, whether it's law, medicine, sales, teaching, coaching, science, or the arts the top people – or those who are headed to the top – are the ones who regularly show up for seminars at their own expense. They read good books and regularly listen to motivational recordings. They deliberately seek information and inspiration and, as a result, they are constantly growing.

Do it Well – Subconsciously?

Why are successful men and women positive? To reverse it, why are positive men and women successful? They're positive because they deliberately feed their minds with good, clean, powerful, positive mental thoughts on a regular basis. They make them a part of their daily diets just as surely as they make food a part of their physical diets. They know that if they feed their bodies above the necks; they'll never have to worry about feeding their bodies below the neck. They won't have to worry about the roof over their heads, or the financial problems often associated with old age. As we dig into the learning process and look at some real life examples it will become obvious why this is true.

Virtually everything we learn, we learn consciously. It's only when we do it subconsciously that we do it well. You learned how to drive a car consciously. Remember? If your car had a clutch, do you remember the instructions you said to yourself? Push in the clutch; press the accelerator, just a little, careful now - push the gearshift lever, now let the clutch out – easy does it - pull the gearshift lever. Do you remember? Do you also remember you would buck up and jump and probably kill the engine?

You were a menace to society and a candidate for the morgue because you were learning to drive consciously. Sometime later, you could press the accelerator, shift the gear, let out on the clutch, and unwrap a piece of gum, roll down the window and talk about a neighbour all at the same time. You could do these things with complete safety because you moved the driving process from the conscious mind into the subconscious mind. You learned to drive consciously and later it became "unconscious" or automatic. It was almost a reflex action.

Every musician – regardless of the instrument – went through the slow and often painful process of learning to consciously play that instrument. During the learning process, friends and relatives studiously avoided listening to the efforts of the aspiring Ignace Paderewski. The musician plays skilfully only when he plays instinctively or subconsciously. Then everyone wants to listen – free, of course.

Do you remember when you learned how to type? You had to concentrate on every stroke as you beat out about ten words per minute. You were typing consciously and you were doing a miserable job. Later, you no longer thought about the key you were going to hit, you just typed. You were then doing it subconsciously and doing it well.

Once you learn to do something consciously, you can move it into the subconscious and do it well. Everything you do well will be done subconsciously. This includes your attitude. You can move your attitude reactions into the subconscious. You can do this so completely you will instinctively react positively to negative situations as well as positive ones. That's a promise. It takes dedication, work and practice, but it can be done. A positive responsive to any stimulus can become something like a reflex-action or a conditioned response.

On the next page you will see an elephant and a baby elephant . I'd like you to take a good look at this picture and then look at yourself in a mirror take a real <u>hard</u> look. Do you see yourself in the same boat as this elephant? If so; break the rope, step out of the rut, and get out of your mould. I know you <u>can</u> <u>do</u> <u>better</u>, <u>don't</u> <u>delay</u>, <u>and start</u> <u>today</u>!

Circus Elephants and Conditioning

An elephant can easily pick up a one ton load with his trunk. But have you visited a circus and watched these huge creatures standing quietly while tied to a small wooden stake?

While still young and weak, an elephant is tied by a heavy chain to an immovable iron stake. No matter how hard he tries, he cannot break the chain or move the stake. Then no matter how large and strong the elephant becomes, he continues to believe he cannot move as long as he can see the stake on the ground beside him. This same conditioning principle takes place with human beings in their personality development.

Flea Trainer

Another way of looking at the reason why you hold yourself back, thus not succeed, is because you were told over the years that you were not good enough, so our brains are out of whack because of your past experiences. Let me give you an idea, why it happened to you!

I was flying back to Toronto, some years ago from Chicago, where I did a motivational speech, as an after dinner guest speaker, as we were flying a gentleman approached me and said "aren't you the man that is the fly trainer"? and I said that I was. You see in my speech the evening before I was telling people about fly training. You see my dear reader, we all should be one.

Let me tell you how it works. I would like you to catch a flea, don't kill it, you need it alive to become a flea trainer!

Now you have this flea, and I want you to put it in a clear glass or plastic jar, then you put a plastic cover on it. Put a few small holes in that cover because the flea needs air, I do not want you to kill it. So here we are, the flea is confined in this jar, you will see this flea go crazy. Jumping up and down, hitting the cover, sits on the wall of the glass etc., etc. This flea will do this for maybe three, four, five hours, then the flea will sit in the bottom of the jar and decide it can't get out, you can at that time remove the cover, and the flea does not get out right away, because it believes it can't get out.

When I tell this story, <u>don't you feel the same as that flea</u>? You tried, tried, and tried again and you did not succeed, because we have been told as a child and as a grown-up we aren't good enough!

Let's get rid of this crap in your head, and become the person you want to be, start today, not tomorrow, today, because this is the first day of the rest of your life.

· CHAPTER 17 ·

Tap – Tap – Tap!

Let's set the stage, I want to call your attention to the powerful effect of repetition or reiteration.

For example, take a pneumatic chisel. You have seen one used in breaking up solid concrete or piercing holes through steel. It's the tap, tap, tap of that chisel with a terrific force behind it, which causes disintegration of the particles and makes a dent or hole in the object on which it is placed.

All of us have heard of the old torture system of dripping water on the forehead. Perhaps you are familiar with Kipling's "Boots". It's the tramp, tramp of boots, boots that makes men mad. It's the constant, never ending repetition that penetrates.

While you may realize how repetition works on material things, you may not thoroughly appreciate the tremendous impression that repetition also makes upon the human mind.

You have long since recognized that the fundamental of advertising is its repetition, its appeal by reiteration:

"It floats......"
"There's a reason......"
"I'd walk a mile......"
"There're kind to the throat......."

"Good to the last drop......."

And so on and so on, over and over!

They shout these slogans at you, sing them, play them, picture them – there's no escape – by constant repetition the advertized merits of each product are dinned into your consciousness until you almost spout slogans in your sleep. Tap – tap – tap – they are beat in upon you every time you turn on your radio or television set or turn the page of a newspaper or magazine, or drive around town, along the highways, you pass billboards that compete against the scenery, crying out: "Look at me! Get my message! Go by me if you will – but, then go buy!" You look up in the sky and a plane passes over, trailing a streamer, "The pause that refreshes" or a skywriter is twisting and turning while he spells out in smoke: "Not a cough in a carload!" On subway trains, streetcars, buses, railroads, steamships, taxicab, automobiles, trucks – on everything that moves, ever on jackasses, you will see signs advertising something. The mighty force of repetition – repetition – repetition! You may have a poor memory, but, you're never permitted to forget an advertised product, even for a day!

Think back, through the "science" of repetition, you learned the alphabet, how to multiply. A-B-C ... two times two are four ... c-a-t spells cat ... tap, tap, tap! Until you've got it – or it's got you!

Everything you've ever memorized was impressed upon your consciousness through repetition. You are constantly (tap, tap, tap) being reminded to reaffirm (more tap, tap) your faith in your religious belief. The same science, again and again, repetition, reiteration, tap, tap, tap.

Arthur Schopenhauser said, "There is no absurdity so palpable but that it may be firmly planted in the human head if you only begin to inculcate it before the age of five, by constantly repeating it with an air of great solemnity.

The connection between the conscious and the subconscious or objective mind is close. Every student of the subject knows what may be accomplished by definitely contacting the subconscious. When you get a specific detailed picture in your conscious mind by using this process of reiteration or repetition, and make the subconscious mind click, you have at your command, the power that astounds.

Skilled prosecutors, clever defenders, appeal to the emotions of the jurors, never to the conscious reason. How do they do it? Simply by the process of repeating and emphasizing, time after time, the points they wish to stress. They do it with usage of words and variations of arguments and tones of voice, dripping with emotion. Behind all there is that tap, tap, tap – tapping the subconscious – making the jurors believe. They've heard it again and again ... it must be so!

It is important to stay with your idea, once you get it and feel that it is right. Repeat it over and over. Get your husband or wife or close friend to visualize with you, if he or she is in harmony and sympathy with your desired objectives. That's how power is generated.

Use the Tap, Tap System!

When you have the picture firmly in your mind, begin using the tap, tap system, as I have outlined. It is going to be the repetition, the reiteration of that picture upon the subconscious mind that will cause the creative power within to produce results for you.

The world's most successful men and women live daily with their ideas. They hold their objectives constantly in mind. It isn't just a case with them of picturing something once, and then forgetting about it. Theirs is not a wishy-washy or dilly-dally approach, they mean business. They expect to reach their goals, they are willing to work day and night if necessary, to get there, and they have faith that this power within is working right along with them, giving them guidance in the form of urges to move in the right direction, magnetizing conditions around them, attracting resources and opportunities in accordance with their needs!

You can measure the intensity of your own desires in comparison. How much of a price in effort and sacrifice are you willing to pay to attain the things you want in life? Are you willing to try to accomplish something over and over again, until by repetition, out of seeming failure, you gain the experience and the ability to achieve? When you are, you must eventually succeed. Nothing can stop you. All obstacles must yield to your will, your drive, your faith, your God-given creative power, when you persist. You must realize at the start that you can't get something for nothing. The universe doesn't operate this way. You must give out in effort and in faith, if you wish to receive.

Tap, tap, tap — visualizing what you want over and over — little drops of water, the endless pounding of the sea on the beach, the tramp, tramp of feet on stone stairs, cause and effect --- cause and effect ... action always brings about reaction. You can't notice it at first, but, the forces of nature and of mind, centered on any obstacle, can move that obstacle in time, or wear it away, or change it.

Harness Your Power to Faith

Faith can move mountains, mountains of fear and doubt and worry, faith repeated again and again – faith in yourself, faith in the God Power within. It's a simple, silent, unspectacular operation, when you view it at any second, but over a long time span, what you accomplish will astound you.

Now, you are the sum total of what you believe, good and bad; what you have accepted in mind, what is motivating your thoughts and acts as a result of your beliefs. As your beliefs change, your life will change with them, for your life is really based upon faith.

You have faith, everyday, that you are going to keep on breathing, that your heart will continue beating, that you are alive and well. If this faith is upset, your health is upset. You have faith in everything around you ... your work, your friends, your ability, your car, your future. You've accepted all this as a part of your life. You visualize a continuance of it all as it has been in the past. Each day you add to the repetition, in general, of another similar experience. You get more and more in the groove of whatever you are doing and this may be bad, if you are doing little that is worthwhile. It can be good if you are applying yourself as you should.

Take inventory and make sure that what you are repeating, day after day, is helping you grow in experience, in ability, in achievement, in personal satisfaction and happiness. If it is not, you will not wish to go on repeating these activities and interests. You may want to break away from them and start a new cycle of development for yourself.

The Process of Getting Ahead Sooner

Remember: what man has done once he will do again, because he is a creature of habit. Bad thoughts are easily repeated because like always attracts like. Whatever thoughts you take into consciousness will not feel at home unless they can find similar thoughts to keep them company. What kind of thoughts are you entertaining? Are they the kind that can lead you to things you don't want to do, to experiences you don't want to have? If they are, throw them out <u>now</u>, before they become deeply entrenched through repetition.

An excessive drinker finds it difficult to stop drinking because the habit of drink has been so long impressed upon body and mind. He "sees" himself taking another drink so vividly that it becomes a gigantic task to picture himself not drinking.

The pictures you hold of yourself in mind today have only to do with your past. If you don't take charge and create new pictures of yourself, you will only repeat tomorrow what you have done today and yesterday.

Most human beings, unhappily, are on a treadmill of their own making, ending up each day where they were yesterday, although seeming to make progress because they have been moving about. The merry-go-round always ends up at the same place unless you take stock of where you are going, get off the rotating platform by visualizing a new direction and purpose in life, and then take the high road toward greater and greater happiness and success, which can never breached on a carousel.

Tap, tap, tap! If the tap, tapping that is going on in your consciousness producing more of the same for you ... or is it the kind of tap, tapping – repetition of pictures – that is impressing right thoughts and right actions upon your subconscious.

You are the only one who knows. You are the only one who can do anything about it! Learn to use the great power of repetition in the right way, and all good things shall be added unto you!

• CHAPTER 18 •

Relaxation with Meditation

During the past few years, the slightly mysterious sounding techniques of meditation have become increasingly popular. Why? What is the value of meditation? The answer is simple; a person who practices meditation gives themselves an opportunity to rest, relax and free themselves from many stress factors. Meditation is a relaxing activity, not a religion or philosophy, as so many tend to think. It can relieve inner tension, improve your physical and emotional health, and it can even help reduce blood pressure, ease depression, increase your energy and brain power and contributes to an overall sense of well being and happiness. When you practice meditation twice a day, for ten minutes each, you allow your thoughts to flow through your conscious mind and you become a passive spectator to your own thoughts, watching them move naturally about your mind without getting involved with what is happening to you at the mental level. The state produced by meditation is free of stress and tensions and you are then able to draw from your natural supply of energy. To meditate you need only four things; a quiet place, an object to think about, a passive attitude and a comfortable position:

1. Sit comfortably, feet on the floor, hands on your lap.
2. Do not allow your hands or feet to touch.
3. Close your eyes. Breath a bit slower.
4. Progressively tell the following parts of your body to relax:

   Toes of left foot..... relax
   Toes of right foot..... relax
   Ankle of left foot..... relax
   Ankle of right foot..... relax
   Lower left leg..... relax
   Lower right leg..... relax
   Upper left leg..... relax
   Upper right leg..... relax
   Groin area..... relax
   Buttocks..... relax
   Stomach..... relax
   Chest..... relax
   Left shoulder..... relax
   Right Shoulder..... relax
   Left arm..... relax
   Right arm..... relax
   Left fingers..... relax
   Right fingers..... relax
   Neck..... relax
   Face..... relax..... now you are completely relaxed all over

5. Listen to your breathing
6. Repeat the word "relax"
7. Try not to let your mind wander
8. After 10 to twenty minutes, take a deep breath
9. Stand up and stretch like a cat. You should feel totally renewed.

When you have <u>learned</u> to lie or sit passively, doing nothing, simply watching your own breathing with detached interest, you will slowly become aware that your body is pervaded by a sensation of calmness. And your harassed feeling of being rushed has slipped away. (Warning!); I say, "when you have learned" because this is not something you can do in the spur of the moment. The fact that you have grasped the idea does not mean that you have achieved the sensation. Relaxation is not something to be read about with the idea that it will work while you sleep. It is something to be experienced. The first few minutes are the hardest because you are trying to learn something in a hurry, to find out what it is all about and then rush on to the next thing. That is natural because your trouble is nervous tension, but after you have watched that gut breathing, and seen that the lift in the abdomen goes lower and lower, that the pause before inhaling is longer, you will begin to lose acute awareness of time. When you have really mastered this technique, a few minutes of this complete rest of mind and body will give you a degree of rest, which formerly requested at least an hour of sleep. Your body will seem like an empty shell through which the oxygen washes like a great wave. Your mind, emptied of sensation, will sink into a king of nirvana in which you will hardly be conscious of your surroundings, in which you will almost forget your own name. This is the state of upper repose, mentally, physically and emotionally. This is what I call meditation. It creates a mood which is an intermediate state between consciousness and sleep, called Alpha Level; in which you forget your daily problems.

· CHAPTER 19 ·

Visualization and Imagination

We noted that the very first step toward personal motivation is to crystallize your thinking so that you know where you stand now and where you are going. But without some further amplification of what is meant by "crystallized thought" your success may fall far short of your expectations. Our world moves at such a rapid pace that much of our thinking is done in vague generalities. We read or we listen to what others have to say with varying degrees of receptivity. The moment our minds grasp a general understanding of one idea, we proceed to the next one. But there is seldom any dialogue that helps fix the outlines of these thoughts with any exact definition or boundary. Our minds do not expand to encompass the whole idea – there just isn't enough time. As a result, our thought is seldom crystallized to the point that we know exactly what we have heard or read. We form the habit of generalizing ideas.

When you resolve to fill out a plan of action for your life – when you begin to analyze where you stand and where you are going – generalizations do not suffice. Your ideas and thoughts must be so vivid and detailed that you are able to spell out every facet of them exactly. You should be able to see not only the goals, but every step you will take to reach them without one moment of hesitation or uncertainty. And the way you achieve this kind of crystallized thinking is through the process of visualization.

In our culture today, virtually all patterns of thought are geared to sight. The simplest thought usually calls forth an image in the mind's eye. Mention a tree and one "sees" a tree. Mention an abstract thought and the mind must grapple with it until it is able, somehow to reduce the abstraction to a mental picture. When people are unable to "get the picture", they are confused and do not understand. Or if they get the wrong picture, they misunderstand. In a very literal sense, that is visualization. In other words, we relate the present to the past by converting current thoughts into mental pictures of our past experiences, and we understand by association. We form a "bridge" by using visualization.

People do not use visualization to their best advantage, however, until they develop the art of visualization in its highest form: that of relating the present to the future. When we are able to use our powers to relate the "what is" to the "what can be" we have developed visualization into a genuine art.

To illustrate that you have the basic ability to visualize, I ask you to think of an automobile. Your mind will picture that idea very quickly. But if you are like most people, the picture you get is rather hazy. If I ask you to describe the automobile you have in mind, you have to go back and refocus the picture because you didn't really know, in the beginning, what to expect. Even when you have a mental picture so clear you can describe the car, it is pretty sure that the car you see is your *own* automobile. That's the way most of us respond to the little events in life. Our minds are lazy and we get by on minimum requirements of effort. We restrict our visualization to that which we already know – to familiar and commonplace. We omit imagination, the spice that adds meaning and zest to our power of visualization.

The successful person – the self motivated person – is not restricted. They have set their imagination free. They know that they can visualize anything that they can create, and can create anything they can visualize. They have found by the process of visualization, they can move the future into the present and greatly expand their own experience. They get already "familiar" with it. They have already "seen" it through visualization.

Almost everyone is adept at bridging the past with the present. That's how we profit from past experiences, and we do so with some confidence and self assurance. But how much more confidence could we gain if we extended our ability and utilized the practice to give us the same understanding of our future action. Vivid imagination makes this kind of visualization possible.

People must be able to unshackle themselves, set emotions free and be willing to sense each experience they visualize. When they can taste, smell, hear, or touch, as well as see, regarding the future, their imagination is most vivid.

The top teaching professionals in the world of golf tell their students that one of the most important secrets of making a golf shot is being able to visualize where you want the ball to go. They stress the importance of seeing tin the mind's eye the exact flight and path of the ball. If one can also hear the click of the ball and feel the smooth flex of the muscles, their chances of making the shot are virtually assured. Why? Because the thought is the data fed into the computer, the brain, and the entire body chemistry gets the message clearly. The muscles respond according to the precise instructions. Timing, body control and swing come almost automatically because visualization had commanded that they respond appropriately. By contrast, if a person is confused – if they don't know which club to use of how they want the shot to look – their computer feeds garbled messages to the muscles and the shot is missed. Anyone who has played the game for a period of years knows this principle to be true. Yet it is not a principle confined to the sports world in general, nor to golf in particular. It is a pragmatic principle available to anyone in any profession, and it is especially effective as you crystallize your thinking about what you want to achieve in life.

Visualization and Belief

All of us are familiar with the old saying "seeing is believing", but that statement was never truer than when it is related to visualization. When people set certain goals, aims and desires, and when they use their power of visualization to picture themselves already in possession of those goals, they develop an almost miraculous belief in themselves and their ability to achieve those goals.

Far too many people make resolutions, or set goals for attitude changes but, rely solely on their willpower to accomplish the objective. Willpower alone will not work because our determination and willpower do not foster belief. Unless we can "see" the end results through visualization, we are forging ahead into the "unknown" and our confidence and belief will not sustain us. The reason so many find it difficult to lose weight or stop smoking, or break any long engrained habit, is because they rely solely on willpower. Remember that habits and attitudes are changed by displacement. People must find a more satisfactory mode of behaviour to replace old habits. This can be done by visualizing already having the new behaviour. This is not to say that determination is unimportant. It is important, as we shall see. It does not provide any new or more satisfactory mode of action, and it does not bolster belief.

The role visualization plays in fostering the belief that attitudes can be changed, prompts us to make a comparison between genuine visualization and daydreams. The two should never be confused because in almost every respect, they are direct opposites. Daydreams are an escape from the pressures of reality. Visualization is a constructive way to meet the challenges of life, head on and overcome them. Daydreams are spawned in the inactive. The daydreamer never intends to take action on their dreams. Those who develop their powers of visualization, do so with purpose. They not only plan to act, they are practicing the art so they may be prepared to act more effectively. The daydreamer does not believe in what they dream. Their dream is only a whim, a wish, a fantasy. Many times they would not even want the dream to come true if they had the power to make it so. The person of vision develops belief, confidence and assurance that what they see is not only possible, but is in fact, in the process of becoming reality. They are on the way, and in a sense, they have already used their power of visualization like the picture editor of a magazine such as Life, Look or National Geographic. They select the picture they want carefully and build the "Story" of their personal development around them. At the same time, they reject and discard those pictures they do not want. Their editorial policy sets out a constructive course of action for them to follow. They learn to distinguish the true from the false, the real from the unreal. When problems and obstacles confront them like a wall, they know that they have only to raise their sights higher to find a way around or over any hindering circumstances. The person who can visualize is well on the way to success because they have seen the progressive realization of their predetermined worthwhile goals.

Visualization and Concentration

In developing the art of visualization, it is not enough simply to free our minds from the restriction of past experiences through the use of a vivid imagination. We must zero in on our goals and plans by exercising our powers of concentration. We have already seen that most of us form the habit of generalizing the thoughts and ideas advanced by others – often because there is no real opportunity to explore an idea in depth with the person who is writing or speaking. There is never a real reason to "generalize" those thoughts or ideas emanating from our own minds. We can, by concentration, explore every facet of our thought until it becomes crystal clear, and we can visualize it exactly.

You may be able to see the importance of such crystallized thinking to the achievement of your goals if you think of your mind as a camera. You take a mental picture of the goal you want to reach. If the camera is ten percent out of focus, the picture will be ten percent tout of focus. There is no way to get a clear photograph from an out of focus camera. There is no way to reach a clearly defined goal until there is a clearly defined mental image of the goal you want to reach.

If you are ten percent "out of focus" in your visualization, the goal will be distorted by ten percent when you reach it. It may be recognizable, but, it is never completely satisfying. You probably know from experience that, when you send film in to be developed, the processors don't even bother to send back a print of your really bad negatives. It's much the same way with goals and objectives. If your visualization is poor and if you have not crystallized your thinking clearly, you will not come anywhere near reaching the goals you have set.

Let's say that in your plans for the future, you've set your sights on having a "dream home". That's one of your long-range tangible goals. Can you describe the home? Most people, when asked that question, will answer yes. They then proceed to tell you how many rooms it has, what the general construction and shape will be and some of the basic materials. If they are questioned further — if they are asked to describe the guest room in detail, or the lot, the landscape, the furniture, the fixtures, or hardware — they begin to get down and become confused. They have never concentrated in that much detail. Their mental camera is still ten, twenty, even fifty percent out of focus. That's why so many people have built their dream house, only to experience a number of disappointments because there were so many minor items they overlooked.

When you give your imagination free reign and begin to visualize your goals and plans with controlled attention and concentrated energy, you will begin to see some startling results.

1. Visualization changes a general idea into something more specific. You bring your mental camera into focus. Things begin to take shape and what before was just a confused blur, becomes a crystal-clear image. Your dream home, for example, can become so real, you can see the roses bloom, the picture on the wall and the view from the bedroom window. Your powers of visualization are able to dispel any apprehension or worry connected with your goals because the unknown becomes known and the indefinite becomes definite.

2. When you use your powers of concentration, you will begin to notice errors and incongruities in your plans, and you'll be able to make corrections before mistakes are made. Again, using the illustration of your dream home, you might find that the floor

plan you envision is wrong for the home site you've selected. The afternoon sun falls on the patio, or the land falls toward the house so that the rainfall drains into the garage instead of away from it. Or, the split-level floor plan you like is not right for the ground slope. You'll even be able to visualize how the inside door should be hung so they don't take up too much valuable wall space when they stand open. Mistakes once made are sometimes difficult to remedy, and regardless of what goals you set, any system that helps you correct errors before they happen is a valuable one. With concentrated visualization, you are able to spot mistakes, adjust and correct them, and then proceed without serious consequences. Your ego gets a big boost in the bargain because you "save face" by eliminating the embarrassment of actually making the mistake.

3. Concentration enables you to see differences as well as similarities. Your first tendency, in trying to visualize your dream home, for example, will probably be to see it as being like some other home you've seen – either in person or in a magazine. If you really concentrate, you'll be able to separate the features you like from those you don't care for. You'll be able to visualize differences as well as similarities and give your home a distinctive touch that carries the flavour of your family's personality.

The examples we have used for concentrated visualization of your dream home are equally applicable to all your goals and plans, including any goals to make the internal changes of attitude. You must be able to "see" yourself as already having the traits or qualities you want to acquire. The thought is precedent to the action. Before we can be, we must become, and before we can become, we must be able to visualize our goals.

The Art of Visualization

1. The term "crystallized thinking" implies definitive shape, content and detail. Thus, no matter what thought is crystallized, its form is unrelieved by any distortions or shadings.

2. We all think in pictures. Even when the thought is a general abstraction such as "happiness" or "fun" we picture a scene to which those words apply.

3. Since time and the passage of time are relative, there is very little difference. The only thing we gain from the past is experience.

4. Visualization stimulates physical reaction as well. An imagined food delicacy makes your mouth water. Every athlete's body prepares for physical action before it happens.

5. Concentration exerts control over visualization. It prevents extraneous thoughts from distorting the picture you hold in your mind. It intensifies deliberate concern.

6. It certainly can. Just s the focus control on a camera can bring a scene into sharp relief, so can you focus your mind on a thought.

7. Willpower alone is determined without a definite goal in sight. Sincere belief "sees" the end result before it happens. Belief is positive expectancy in action.

8. An extremely important part. Goals, whether long-range or short-range, can't exist until we visualize them as tangibles. We can't strive for something that defies description.

9. Comparable, but not at all similar. A daydream is a wish-fantasy visualization is a determined projection into reality. We visualize what can be, no matter how improbable it may seem.

10. Every goal is a conscious and determined intent. If you arrive at a destination you've never thought of or heard about, it can't possibly be your goal.

• CHAPTER 20 •

Something to Think About

There was a young woman who had been diagnosed with a terminal illness and had been given three months to live. So, she was getting her things "in order", she contacted her pastor and had him come to her house to discuss certain aspects of her final wishes.

She told him which songs she wanted sung at the service, what scriptures she would like read, and what outfit she wanted to be buried in.

Everything was in order and the pastor was preparing to leave when the young woman suddenly remembered something very important to her.

"There's one more thing" she said excitedly.

"What's that" came the pastor's reply.

"This is very important" the young women continued, "I want to be buried with a fork in my right hand".

The pastor stood looking at the young woman, not knowing quite what to say.

"That surprises you, doesn't it" the young woman asked.

"Well, to be honest, I'm puzzled by the request" said the pastor.

The young woman explained "my grandmother once told me this story, and from that time on I have always tried to pass along its message to those I love and those who are in need of encouragement. In all the years of attending socials and dinners, I always remembered that when the dishes of the main course were being cleaned, someone would inevitably lean over and say, "keep your fork" it was my favourite part because I knew that something better was coming ... like velvety chocolate cake or deep dish apple pie, something wonderful, and with substance.

So, I just want people to see me there in that casket with a fork in my right hand and I want them to wonder. "<u>What's</u> <u>with</u> <u>the</u> <u>fork</u>"? Then I want you to tell them: "Keep your fork, the best is yet to come."

The pastor's eyes welled up with tears of joy as he hugged the young woman good-bye. He knew this would be one of the last times he would see her before her death. But he also knew that the young women had a far better grasp of "after life" than he did. She had a better understanding that "life" does not stop at our physical death, our spirit lives forever. She <u>knew</u> that something better was coming.

At the funeral people were walking by the young woman's casket and they saw the clothes she was wearing and fork placed in her right hand. Over and over, the pastor heard the question "What's with the fork?" and over and over he smiled.

During his message, the pastor told the people of the conversation he had with the young woman shortly before she died. He also told them about the fork and about want it symbolized to her. He also told the people how he could not stop thinking about the fork and told them that they probably would not be able to stop thinking about it either.

He was right, so the next time you reach down for your fork let it remind you, ever so gently, that the best is yet to come.

Friends are a very rare jewel. They make you smile and encourage you to succeed.

They lend an ear, they share a word of praise, and they always want to open their hearts to us. Show your friends how much you care. Remember to always be there for them, even when you need them more. For you never know when it may be their time to "Keep your fork".

Cherish the time you have, and the memories you share. Being friends with someone is not an opportunity but a sweet responsibility!

· CHAPTER 21 ·

Motivational/Inspirational Living

Some years ago I was in Paramus, New Jersey on a speaking engagement about motivational and inspirational living. The day following the workshop, I spent some time in a beautiful mall with trees, waterfalls and nice things to see. It was very modern, with background music, (I love music) plus gorgeous decorations. I was having a coffee and a snack in the food court, when a couple approached me, they introduced themselves and mentioned that they had attended my presentation the evening before and really enjoyed the evening.

After a motivational/inspirational speech, people want to talk to me personally, about their own experiences, or lack thereof. Jim (not his real name) and his wife had no chance to talk to me that evening, because I was to busy, Jim decided to write to me instead. But meeting me by change made his day. He told me a story about his experience in his life with a great setback, that gave him a new, better and happier life. "When I was 51 years old, Jim said, I had a major heart attack. I was Vice-President of a major company at that time and after great medical care I came through this set back. The doctors saved my life, and they told me not to go back to this pressure cooking job, to avoid another attack".

"I used to have a busy active life, with the job and our social life. I became very bored and restless with my life, doing nothing but doctors appointments and medication. My sweetheart wife must have had a bad time with me, I became a grumpy old man."

Some of my friends kept telling me to find something to do, find a hobby, they came up with all kinds of ideas, but nothing turned me on. One of my friends suggested, take up painting. I didn't know how to hold a brush or a pallet but finally decided to take lessons. I had to do something, the walls drove me nuts.

My friend found me an instructor, and off I went for my first lesson on a Monday afternoon. I was nervous but also excited, because finally after many months I had somewhere to interest to go.

When I came home my lovely wife asked "Jim how was it?" I said, "I felt kind of strange and excited at the same time, but I felt great". The class consisted of seven students and I went there once a week and practiced at home a bit. After about 10 lessons the teacher took me aside and said to me that he could not teach me anymore and that I was a natural artist. He told me to go out there and paint.

"Well Jack", he said "that was the big turnaround in my life. In your speech the other night you said, when God closes one door, He will open a window, how true it is."

Jim started to paint, gave some paintings away and also sold some paintings. In about a year he was making a good living from his new career. As a matter of fact, Jim and his misses sold their home and bought a good size RV and travelled the USA and South America. They followed the sun. They didn't like winter anymore and had always wanted to travel, but never did, because of the position he had before.

Of course Jim paints when they park the RV and spends a week or two in the same place. Jim has four art shows a year, in the same cities at the same time each year, where they sell all the art Jim makes. They both agreed that they are happy, very contented and making a good living, and both of them look like they are in their mid-forties but really are in their mid fifties. And then Jim said to me, "I wish my heart attack had come sooner. I wasted a lot of my prime years."

When you are driving a car, and you find the road blocked, you find yourself looking for another way to get to your destination, which is what happened with Jim and his wife. They found a way around their roadblock. What I am saying is you can find a way around your problems, I know you can do it.

Free Cruises

Most people love to travel but only wish along and very seldom get anywhere. I am like you and love to travel. The difference between you and I is that travel became my priority. I took steps that you don't want to take.

First I became a member of a pen-pal club with head offices in Australia. Within a month, I was writing letters (no e-mail) to fourteen people all over the world some were singles and some were families. Next thing I did was to get rid of my car and travel by public transit and out of town by Greyhound (Bus). A car cost about five to six thousand dollars a year. So instead of putting out all that money on a car, I travel and have seen about one third of this great world of ours.

People form Chilli, Indonesia, Philippines, South Korea, etc., visited me for three to four weeks CN Tower Harbour Front, North Bay and the French River. In return, I got to go to all these places and my new friends showed me their countries.

We all paid our own airfares (I love to fly) but we saved piles of money on hotel and meal costs. We always shared some of the cost so everybody was happy and I made friends all over the globe. My Christmas cards are from all over the place. This chapter is called Free Cruises and the following is an exciting story.

As I said before, I love to travel. So, I read travel stories in magazines and newspapers to learn how people in other countries live and what they have to offer. Of course, my pen pals sent me some interesting information as well. I am also a newspaper reader from cover to cover. I read an interesting story in the Toronto Star, it read "retired and semi-retired men wanted and needed as hosts on cruise ship". This was exciting so I called the cruise line in California. They sent me a number of forms to fill out. I sent them back for their evaluation. About three weeks later, a letter arrived inviting me to come to the office for an interview. Off I went to California. It went marvellously well and they explained that the duties were to mostly keep the unattached ladies and widows busy on the dance floor. Wow! What a job. And that suited me just fine as I love dancing and had a dance club once in Toronto called Club La Vie (as you have already read about). The cruise line was called Royal Cruise Lines. They still exist but have been sold. As far as I know, all the better cruise lines do the same things now, take on retired and semi-retired men to keep the ladies dancing. I went for two cruises, each two weeks in duration on the Adriatic Sea. That sea is between Italy and the southern part mainland Europe. Both Ships were just gorgeous. The food and service was superb with Las Vegas style entertainment. Of course, we went on shore during the day and sailed at night. I was in Greece, Turkey, Yugoslavia, Rome Florence, Venice and France. It was a great experience, I will never forget this wonderful time in my life.

You have to make priorities. What do you need in life to make you happy? I am teaching you a science that will work for you, with your job, career, family, etc. You may say it is easy for me to talk, well, it was not easy for me either until I took this science seriously. That was when things started to change. They will change for you all you have to do is the work.

· CHAPTER 22 ·

My Own Sanctuary

When I was a youngster I had a very special friend, as I was growing up, I was in need of a very good and close friend.

I am the youngest of seven brothers and sisters, and that makes a large family, my parents were great parents, my mother was an angel in disguise, when she talked to you about life, you listened and listened well, she was always making sense, even in difficult situations. She was a loving caring person and I always feel blessed to have had her as a mother and teacher of life "May God Bless her Soul".

My dad was a hard working man, he set the rules and you followed. He was a strict man, but also very, very fair, he didn't go around beating us up, but if you refused to listen to reason, you may have ended up with a hand on your behind. What else do you do when you have seven children to raise? Our family had a meeting every two or three weeks, today you would call it a (family meeting) pow-wow, we could say what (bothered us) beefs we had, things were talked about not screamed about, and the lives of all of us were good and we took great care for each other, and I felt loved, listened to and appreciated.

· JACK DEURLOO ·

Let me go back to this great friend of mine, it was a beautiful tree, and he was the harbour in my storms. I am sure that when you were growing up, and did not understand grown up things, that you could go to somewhere and find that inner peace and trust, well I found this in my friend the tree.

I would run to my tree, down the river road, and along the riverbank, there grew a tall magnificent tree with low branches that hung over the rapid moving river.

The minute my hands touched the bark of my tree, I could feel this wonderous feeling of peace come all over me, I would crawl and climb to the centre of the big branches and sit there in peace, hidden within the branches and leaves.

I always liked and loved nature. I loved to work in my mother's garden. When I was a child I also loved animals as pets but also loved farm animals.

The Second World War came into my life at the ripe old age of fourteen, and the next five years were terrible years, with bombs, planes, shootings, killings, strange mean soldiers, hunger etc., etc.

I was very fortunate that I was never really hungry, though I remember my mother saying "Jack, you have had enough," at times, when food was lacking (not her fault).

During those years of stress, my great friend, my tree and I grew closer as pals. I used to climb in the tree with a great sense of protection and tranquility. I would feel the rough bark with my hands and face and told my tree "I love you" and it was as if soothing waves of harmony and peace emanated to me from my dear friend.

The five war years were a living hell and I myself was a soldier from 1945 to 1949 defending our own colony, Indonesia. These years were all very difficult but it taught me one valuable lesson and that is discipline. I have a great sense of value. Please be happy with what you have. I have been here and there, I have done this and that, I have friends in all kinds of countries and have seen one-third of the world, and still say "Canada is the best country in the world", and am very grateful that I emigrated here about sixty years ago now.

My friend, slow down this head of yours, stop spinning, think things over, make peace with yourself, learn mediation and you will find a peaceful living!

Conclusion: My Comment to You!

There is something missing in my life, but I don't know what it is? I want to move forward but I'm stuck! I know I have to make changes, but I'm overwhelmed, scared and alone!

How do I take the first step? This book gives you the guidance, to change the above!

You can have anything you want when you want it passionately enough, your inner passion will create the energy to give you this new world of yours, just believe in yourself.

I told you about Brian and Linda and their home! I told you about Jim who became an artist after a heart attack! I told you about my own free cruises! I told you about my travels! I told you how to get any legal parking space etc., etc.

Change your thoughts, change your life, but you may be a person who "takes care", people who "take care" never get "anywhere" "take a chance", "take charge" and "take control".

I really want you to succeed in your life, I want you to read Chapter 14 – "Science" again, I told you about the six cards, and that they work 100% of the time. I want you to get back to the dictionary again and find the work "affirmation" and it will say something like this "a statement of fact", the answer is in affirmation, positive in manner, a positive plan affirmed.

When you are doing affirmations you are influencing the thought that occurs in your mind, your mind can only think one thought at a time, so affirmations work by filling your mind with thoughts that support your goal.

When your six cards are properly placed you will see them 30, maybe 40 times a day, so each time you see your well placed card, you say or think an affirmation as many times as you see your card.

Here are some affirmations you could use:
Life is golden and sunny, I relax about money
Do it, do it now
Open my door, I am ready for more
Find a need and fill it
I do my best and pass the test
I will persist, yes I can
I see my car, It's mine, I know
Everyday in everyway, I am getting better and better
I will have my trip, it makes me flip
My load is gone, let it begone always
Today is the first day, of the rest of my life!
Relax my mind, let go, unwind
My back is straight, I just can't wait
I am happy and free, accept me.

The above are some samples, you can make then yourself, make them positive and expect things to happen! Affirmation is "a statement of fact".

The answer is in affirmation, positive in manner

Any plan for positive affirmation believe in yourself and your plan.

Enjoy!

CPSIA information can be obtained at www.ICGtesting.com
Printed in the USA
236893LV00001B/13/P